Traveling While Married

Also by Mary-Lou Weisman

My (Middle-Aged) Baby Book: A Record of Milestones,
  Millstones and Gallstones

Intensive Care: A Family Love Story

Traveling While Married

BY
Mary-Lou Weisman

ILLUSTRATED BY
Edward Koren

ALGONQUIN BOOKS OF CHAPEL HILL   2003

Published by
Algonquin Books of Chapel Hill
Post Office Box 2225
Chapel Hill, North Carolina 27515-2225

a division of
Workman Publishing
708 Broadway
New York, New York 10003

Portions of this book have appeared in slightly different versions in the
following publications: "Traveling While Married," *The New York Times*
Travel Section (July 21, 1999); "The Modified Marital Plan," *The New York
Times* Travel Section (Feb. 20, 2000); "Packing," *The New York Times* Travel
Section (Nov. 8, 1998); "Shopping," *European Travel & Life* (Sept./Oct. 1983);
"His Vacation," *The New York Times* Travel Section (June 11, 1989); "Her
Vacation," *New Woman* (Nov. 1991); "Fantasy Real Estate," *The New York
Times* Travel Section (July 9, 2000); "Reality Real Estate," *The New York
Times* Travel Section (Jan. 16, 1994); "The Summer House Guest,"
The New Republic (Sept. 19 and 26, 1983); "A Walk on the Wild Side,"
The New York Times (March 1, 1998).

Library of Congress Cataloging-in-Publication Data
Weisman, Mary-Lou.
Traveling while married / by Mary-Lou Weisman;
illustrated by Edward Koren.—1st. ed.
p. cm.
ISBN 1-56512-319-0
1. Married people—Travel.   I. Title.
G151.W428 2003
910.4'086'55—dc21   2003040402

10   9   8   7   6   5   4   3   2   1
First Edition

To the women in my life, for their
friendship, encouragement, and advice:
Mary Kay Blakely, Liz Brondolo, K. C. Cole,
Nan Dale, Carole Levine, Monica Holmes,
Janet Neipris, Lucie Prinz, Brett Somers,
and Phyllis Theroux.

I, Mary-Lou, take thee, Larry,
to be my constant traveling companion,
to Hong and to Kong, in Cyclades
and in Delft, for deck class or deluxe,
so long as we both can move.

Contents

I am grateful to my agent Rosalie Siegel for her enthusiasm and hard work, and to my editor Elisabeth Scharlatt, whose vision helped to shape this book and whose good humor made work seem like play.

Traveling While Married

Travel can put extra strain on a marriage. Being the same old couple in a new and different place is a disorienting experience. All too often, when people don't know where they are, have jet lag, don't speak the language, and can't figure out the money or maintain intestinal regularity, they get hostile. And since they don't know anybody else in Kyoto to take it out on, they take it out on each other. Because couples therapy is rarely available on vacation, it's important to be aware in advance of the special challenges associated with traveling while married.

Some marriages are saved by going on vacation.

While the marriage is at home, the partners may be contemplating divorce, but send that marriage on vacation and they're on a second honeymoon. On the other hand, a marriage that gets along swimmingly at home can be a fish out of water on vacation.

The very concept of vacationing can mean different things to each partner. My husband, Larry, likes to move around a lot, preferably from place setting to place setting. Food's not that important to me. I like renting other people's homes in Tuscany or

London and then pretending I'm living their life. Unfortunately, I have a talent for choosing people with disastrous lives.

Does a vacation have to have palm trees? Does it have to be far away? (It should be if it's a summer beach house and there's the slightest chance that you will be unable to restrain yourselves from inviting friends to visit.) Should it be in the city or the countryside? Does it involve mostly standing up or lying down? Does it mean getting to throw your clothes all over the room? Does it mean setting the alarm clock for 7:00 A.M. and seeing every museum and monument whether you want to or not? Or does *vacation* mean sleeping until you wake up, dressing slowly to CNN, lingering over a buffet breakfast and an American newspaper, and spending the three remaining daylight hours meandering and otherwise soaking up the atmosphere, usually by mouth? Does it mean calling the office?

Just deciding where to go on vacation can often test the marriage's flexibility. One partner wants to do something physical and adventurous, like trying to outrun molten lava down a volcano; the other prefers something more restful, even spiritual, like raking gravel in a Buddhist monastery. Taking turns is only fair—this vacation, run down the volcano; next year, rake.

Negotiating what time to leave for the airport can be even trickier. I think we need to leave enough time to get lost at least once, run out of gas, and get stuck in traffic. I also emphasize the distinct possibility that my dental work might set off the security alarm and they'll have to do a strip search, for which we need to add on at least another ten minutes. Larry prefers the excitement of the photo finish. Dashing down the gangway as they're rolling it away from the fuselage is his idea of "right on time." The inevitable, mutual rage with which we be-

gin each trip only helps us to appreciate better the good times that lie ahead.

Neatness counts when you're traveling married. Often husband and wife have different comfort levels with regard to orderliness. We've resolved ours. The minute I enter a hotel room, I mentally divide it into "his" and "her" sides. I stake out my side of the room, my side of the bed, and my night table, where I put my book and my watch and my key to the room and anything else I want to be able to find.

I carefully unpack, hang up my clothing in my half of the closet, and put the foldable items in my allotment of large and small bureau drawers. Then I go into the bathroom and line up my pharmaceuticals on my half of the glass shelf, most of which, it may come as no surprise, are prescription

drugs meant to relieve anxiety and obsessive-compulsive behaviors.

Meanwhile, while helping himself lavishly from the minibar, Larry is tossing belts over the back of his chair, emptying the contents of his pockets on his night table, abandoning shirts on his lampshades, and dropping wet towels on his side of the bed.

Travel, for all its spontaneous joys, can disrupt a couple's lifelong routines. Waiting until 11:00 P.M. to have dinner in Madrid is one thing; waiting to use the bathroom in your own hotel room when you're supposed to be on vacation is quite another. A four-bedroom, two-and-one-half bath colonial marriage can crack under the pressure. What kind of lower intestinal droit du seigneur makes him feel entitled to go first *and* bring a book?

Issues of responsibility are especially exacerbated when couples stray far from home. We know who pays the bills and does the dishes at our house, but who's in charge of coming up with the right amount of euros for the bellhop? Who remembers, or forgets, to buy a battery for the camera? Who remembers film? Who takes the pictures? Who fills out the customs card, including flight number? Who has to retrieve the tickets from her backpack in the overhead bin to tell him the flight number? Who gets the film developed? Who, if anyone, ever puts the photos in the album?

Vacationing couples should recognize their individual strengths and weaknesses and make the best of them. I, for instance, have a difficult enough time finding my way around my own hometown, never  mind somebody else's arrondissement. I'm also no good at figuring out money. I can barely deal with the coins in my own realm, although the introduction of the euro has at least standardized my confusion. This is a congenital problem—a matter of being born with a left brain the size of a chickpea—and has nothing whatsoever to do with some Gilliganesque theory about how girls grow stupid at puberty in order to make men feel superior.

When it comes to making his way in foreign

lands, Larry *is* superior. He always knows where he is and how to get where he's going, even if he's never been there before. Anyone in her right mind would relax and enjoy it instead of insisting upon taking the metro in exactly the wrong direction just because she's a feminist.

Sociologists have observed that men tend to stop talking when they get married. They take this penchant for muteness with them when they travel. A woman's efforts to bring her husband out of his shell with "How was your day?" might jump-start him at the dinner table at home, but it won't work on vacation because you've both had the same day.

In anticipation of such a circumstance, many couples choose to travel with another couple; others hope for a chance encounter with a couple they know from home, or a couple they don't know from home, or a couple they know but don't particularly like from home. It doesn't matter. Embrace them enthusiastically. Invite them to join you for dinner.

The introduction of a new female and another alpha male into the dinner-table society causes the men to revert to their talkative, flirty, funny pre-marital selves. What a delightful evening! What a nice couple they are! What a nice couple we are! You decide to get together when you both get home.

You can either arrange to meet this couple again the next day, or you can say good-bye and part. It doesn't matter. Either you'll talk to them at dinner, or you'll have them to talk about at dinner.

Perhaps for totemic reasons, people like to possess a piece of the country they are visiting. Women like to wear it. Men like to eat it. This atavistic urge tends to turn husbands into suffering cartoon characters, sitting on benches outside of foreign dress shops. The wives, for their part, morph into the international food police — "Do you have any idea how many grams of fat are in that cassoulet?"

A successful vacation often depends upon a couple's willingness to commit mutual enabling. "You look gorgeous! Buy it," is Larry's line. Mine is, "Let's have dessert."

The vacation's over. You're in the terminal; the bags are checked. If the marriage can make it through the airport shops, you're home duty-free. Traveling while married has given you the opportunity to share moments of rare intimacy that you might never have enjoyed had you stayed at home—like sex. Buckle up, settle back, and relax. A marriage is at its best at an altitude of thirty-five thousand feet on its way home from vacation.

Why We Travel

"The sole cause of man's unhappiness," Pascal wrote in his *Pensées,* "is that he does not know how to stay quietly in his room." If we were not tempted to venture out, we would never have to experience the disappointments inherent in travel: that arch is not so triumphant; that tower's not so leaning; that *Mona*'s not so *Lisa*.

The fault is not in the three-star sights but in ourselves, that we are the same underlings we were when we were at home—just as prone to boredom, anxiety, and petty thoughts, in spite of the radical change of scene. I can be just as unhappy in front of the rose window at Chartres as I am at my kitchen sink. In fact, I can be more unhappy because I believe I should be happier.

The fact that we bring ourselves wherever we go does not keep us from going. The urge to "get away" may be bred in the bone. Perhaps someday researchers will discover a gene for it. My guess is that they'll find it somewhere between the ones for manic depression and attention deficit disorder.

At the very least, going away is how we fix up our lives so they're worth living when we get back, a procedure not unlike preparing to die. Larry pays bills, stops the mail at the post office, and replaces burned-out lightbulbs. I cancel the newspaper delivery service, recycle the diet soda cans, clean the slime out of the refrigerator drawers, take any items of clothing each of us hasn't worn for two years to Goodwill, and call our friends and family to say good-bye.

Larry and I travel in different but complimentary ways. I travel the way I cook. I follow directions like a fascist. I measure precisely. I don't improvise and I don't make substitutions. If the recipe calls for a pinch of salt, I'm plunged into panic: how many grains are in a pinch? Before we leave for any trip, I read the travel guides slavishly, like a student studying for an exam. I underline. I clip articles. I talk to people who've been there. By the time we leave, I have a file folder full of required sights to see, recommended routes to follow, and places to eat. It's the travel equivalent of preheating the oven to 350 degrees, taking out all the ingredients, and measuring them into tiny bowls, arranged in sequential order.

Larry will not be bullied by travel guides. He likes to wander around without any particular destination, allowing his interest to settle wherever it may. He notices chimney pots, doors on unimportant buildings, and children playing in hidden courtyards. When we were in Ireland, he fell so in love with the town of Kinvara and its people that we never got to Dublin.

We are prompted to travel by different desires. What I look for in a vacation is a place that's as blatantly different from my real life as possible. I want to get carried away. When I set foot upon foreign soil, I don't want to see Blockbuster Video, Pizza Hut, Bed, Bath, or even Beyond. I like my countries backward. I want cows in the streets, minor uprisings, and people who think I'm stealing their soul when I take their picture. I like to vacation among people who wear costumes: grass skirts, wooden shoes, lederhosen, lace hats—I don't care, just as long as they don't resemble me and they live under circumstances with which I am totally unfamiliar, like poverty, dictatorship, or no dining room.

I'm also crazy about rubble. If there must be buildings, then at least let the plaster be peeling and the streets unpaved. I wish all of Rome looked like the Colosseum except for my hotel.

I thrive on cheap thrills. The sight of a woman beating her wash on a rock makes my heart sing. It's not that I begrudge her a washer-dryer. As far as I'm concerned she can have all the large and small appliances imaginable, break through the corporate glass ceiling, and become the CEO of a Fortune 500 if that's what she wants. Just not during my vacation.

I am nostalgic for a world that probably never existed except on the large canvas map that my grammar school teacher would pull down over the

blackboard when it was time for geography lessons. Each country on the map was illustrated with a little girl or boy my age, dressed in the native costume, standing next to something emblematically local. As a result, when I go to Alaska, I want to see igloos and Eskimos chewing blubber. When I go to the Congo I expect to see a little African boy in a loincloth shooting poison blow darts from a dugout canoe. In the Netherlands, which used to be Holland, I search for windmills and girls in wooden shoes and white hats that turn up at the ends. I want Hans Brinker skating on a frozen canal. This means that no matter where I go, I carry with me, in addition to an increasingly large bag of pharmaceutical impedimenta, an impossibly nostalgic dream.

Instant disappointment is the price I pay for my overblown expectations. The airport in Prague looks like any other airport. The taxis in Italy have meters — just like in New York. What was I thinking? That my luggage and I would be borne by chariot into Rome? Along the road from the airport in London shreds of plastic trash bags cling to clumps of scraggly grass, and a billboard flashes great white teeth surrounded by wet red lips clamping down on a hot dog with everything. I might as well be in Trenton. Fortunately, within minutes I make a quick adjustment, downshifting to reality. Suddenly the most mundane details make me swoon with delight—the unfamiliar typeface on the signage in the London tube; the way the Irish build walls by stacking the stones vertically; the impenetrable hedgerows of Cornwall; the wisteria along a ledge in Istanbul.

Larry is a student of history, which is another one of the reasons he loves to travel. He wants to see the places he's read about. Most especially, Larry is a devotee of British naval history and in particular of Vice Admiral Lord Nelson. He has read everything he can find about his hero. Recently, having read all the biographies, some more than once, he's been reduced to reading young-adult fiction on the subject, in addition, of course, to the bulletin published by the Nelson Society, an international organization with headquarters in Yorkshire, of which Larry is card-carrying member number 2379.

For his sixtieth birthday I surprised him with a visit to Portsmouth, where HMS *Victory*, the ship that Nelson commanded during the decisive Battle of Trafalgar, lies at permanent anchor. Affixed to the deck is a brass plaque that reads HERE NELSON FELL. We pause for a moment of silence. Then we repair below deck to view another plaque: HERE NELSON DIED. Standing just inches from where his hero expired, Larry's voice comes close to cracking when he repeats Nelson's last words: "Thank God, I have done my duty."

Then we're off to the National Maritime Museum at Greenwich, a place famous for mean time and for the fact that Lord Nelson's bloody uniform from the Battle of Trafalgar is there on display.

Unlike me, Larry does not need a country to hit him over the head with pyramids, patriarchy, volcanoes, and crenellated castles to make him feel as if he's on vacation. If I travel for a change of scene, Larry travels for a change of self. Like a chameleon, he takes on the protective coloration of his environment and becomes at one with his surroundings. Upon crossing the border, he understands the money, he knows how to use public transportation and where the truck drivers eat. He can find his hotel. He can drive on the left, on the right, or in Palermo. It's as if he were a member of some international witness protection program. He even speaks the language fluidly, if incorrectly.

"Ma femme est ancienne," he told the French pharmacist when we were in Paris on our honeymoon and I was pregnant *(enceinte)* and suffering from morning sickness.

"I'm sorry," the pharmacist replied in perfect English. "We have nothing for that."

When he sticks to the basic "Hello," "Good-bye," and "Where's the toilet?" he usually gets it right. In 1992, while walking down the streets of Kyoto, Larry, this Zelig of travel, greeted every passerby with a deferential bow from the waist and a cheery *"Konnichiwa,"* as if he owned the place. In Turkey the bar mitzvah boy from Philadelphia pressed his hands together and murmured, *"Salaam aleikum,"* to other Muslims.

When he's not speaking the language of the country, he speaks English haltingly and with a slight accent—even to me. "Would you care to . . . um . . . er . . . how you say—have dinner?"

I envy him this talent. When I was a kid, I used to emerge from Saturday afternoon matinees at the Loews Poli having been thoroughly transformed into a fiery Elizabeth Taylor or a tragic Deborah Kerr. After *Roman Holiday* I swanned about the streets of Bridgeport, flashing my dazzling smile, widening my soft doe eyes, and enchanting every passerby with an adorable "Hullo." Sometimes I could hang on to being Audrey Hepburn for as long as twenty minutes before the real me intruded.

Larry has retained that talent into adulthood. Although in real life he cannot enter a room without bruising some part of his body on the doorjamb, after viewing an old Cary Grant movie he's practically balletic. He threads his way nimbly through the crowded theater lobby and exits to the street with catlike grace, or at least he thinks he does.

In countries where people sit in cafés, he sits in cafés. He drinks whatever they do, and when he falls off the smoking wagon—which he invariably does whenever he becomes a foreigner—he smokes their brand. When they ride horses, he does too.

While visiting an old ranch outside of Cuzco, I saw him leap onto a horse, lift his sombrero in a mighty "Hi-yo," and go riding off into the Peruvian sunset. I didn't even know he knew how to ride a horse. If we went to Egypt, he'd probably start walking sideways.

I think one of the reasons that Larry will not travel with a group or hire a guide is that it interferes with his illusion that he's a native. He doesn't want to be told how tall a building is, when it was built, whether or not it's the highest of its kind, how long it took to build it, or how many rocks from what quarry. Do New Yorkers want to know the height of the Empire State Building? When we were in Sicily, Larry didn't need to take the bus up Mount Etna. To a Sicilian, lava is a normal part of life.

We also travel to fall in love again. Travel can make or break a marriage; it restores ours. We have long philosophical discussions. We taste each other's food. We run holding hands. We sing in the car. It usually takes about six months for the salutary effects of the last trip to wear off entirely, for Larry to get sick of his clients, and me of my work, and we of each other. It's time to go away on another vacation, or if not a vacation, then maybe a trial separation.

I can't stand the way he coughs.

He can't stand the way I play with my hair.

It really annoys me that he'll get up in the middle of dinner to change a lightbulb.

It annoys him that I call him compulsive.

He doesn't like it when I say, "You know what?" before I tell him something, when he obviously doesn't "know what," since I haven't told him yet.

I don't like the way he's always talking to me from another room.

He doesn't like the way I tell him things to say while he's on the phone.

I complain that we never talk.

He doesn't think we ever shut up.

I think he's withholding.

He thinks I'm an endless pit of need.

After one vacation, we found each other's company so pleasant that we resolved on the return flight to have a lunch date at a nice restaurant every Wednesday. That particular commitment didn't last a week, since both of us forgot to put it in our calendars when we got home.

Having traveled initially to get away, ultimately we travel to come home. Of course it's exciting to vacation in Paris, Rome, or Kathmandu, but we are tired. We are sick of our clothes. We want our own bed. We are also eager to put into effect the life-enhancing resolutions we've made while we've been gone. Where else but from afar can we see ourselves for what we really are—two hamsters on the wheel of life, Larry a harassed lawyer, and I a lonely, isolated writer? How else but from a considerable distance could it dawn on us that Larry, who perennially mistakes himself for mellow, would be so much happier running a bed-and-breakfast in Vermont than a law firm in Connecticut, and that I could have lots of people to talk to all day long simply by getting a degree in psychology and becoming a therapist, the kind that gets to talk to her clients and tell them what to do? And when else but upon our return could we relish the heightened sense of life's possibilities our resolutions have brought us?

We often experience these moments of truth while flying home, but it can't be the altitude that gives such unfettered, giddy scope to our imaginations; the cabins are pressurized, after all, and besides, we've had the same life-changing revelations coming home from vacation on a train or even in a car.

Most people attribute this phenomenon to "a change in perspective," but I don't think that's it. What Neil Armstrong experienced when he saw the planet Earth from the Moon was a change in perspective. What we experience after being away for two weeks is more like temporary insanity. The condition lasts about a week after our return, usually not long enough for either of us to quit our jobs, sell our house, or get any further than sending away for graduate school catalogs.

Although we have never outgrown our need for resolutions, they are subject to constant change. For one thing, we've dropped some repeat resolutions from the list because we've resolved them so often that even we are embarrassed. How often, after all, can I return from France and not register for a Berlitz course?

We've also noticed that as we've gotten older, our resolutions have devolved from the cosmic to the trivial:

> Become entirely different people
> Live in another country
> Buy a farm
> Move out of the suburbs into the city
> Become vegetarians
> Take adult education courses
> Use the living room more
> Arrange the books in alphabetical order, or at least by categories
> Watch less television
> Keep in touch with nice people we met on the trip

Forty years ago, en route from a vacation, Larry resolved to chuck the law and go to graduate school in English literature. Now, his resolve is more along the lines of not taking any more divorce clients, wearing sports clothes to the office, and being sure he gets a retainer up front. I'm still a writer. My most recent resolution is to locate other lonely writers and go out to lunch with them.

Our tendency to make increasingly modest resolutions might be an indicator of impending maturity, but I doubt it. The point is not the degree of difficulty of the resolution itself—we never do anything we resolve anyway, whether ambitious or modest. The fact that within a week of our return we invariably resume our rotary rodent lifestyle does not mean we have suffered a defeat or that we have learned our lesson. We will never learn our lesson. Resolutions spring eternal. In a few months we'll be off to get ourselves some new ones.

Traveling Poor

Our first sanctified vacation was our honeymoon. It was the early sixties. We were in our early twenties. Larry had just finished his second year of Columbia Law School. I was working at a glamour job in a New York publishing house, making $62.50 a week.

Our three-month-long European honeymoon was sponsored by the generosity of our wedding guests. Instead of giving us multiple teak ice buckets, cheese trays, and revolving fondue sets, they pooled their money and slipped us a check for $1,500.00. "Have fun," read the note.

Our hope was that by camping and cooking most

of our meals, we could make the money last until September, when Larry would begin his last year of law school, but we couldn't, which is why we found ourselves traveling deck-class on a Greek liner that carried passengers between Piraeus and Haifa. Our plan was to work on a kibbutz for the rest of the summer, in exchange for room and board.

We had just delighted in a dinner of tuna from a can, fresh tomatoes, bread, and cheap wine, which we shared with about fifty other deck-class passengers, who shared their dinners with us. A few of them spoke English. Mostly we passed around a lot of wine and sang a lot of international folk songs about oppressed people who never went to college.

Exhausted from trying to speak in tongues, Larry and I bedded down in one of the lifeboats that were cantilevered over the Aegean. All was peaceful. We were snug in our sleeping bags, bathed in starlight, staring at the night sky and listening to the sea.

What, I wondered, was the matter with all those middle-aged tourists below deck, sleeping in beds, living in rooms, eating at tables, getting led around like sheep? Didn't they know they were missing the whole point of travel, getting to know the people and their culture? Didn't they understand that tours, interpreters, guides, and itineraries made it almost impossible for anything genuine to happen? Didn't they realize how their money actually insulated them from the very travel experiences they craved?

"Someday, when we're older," I said to Larry, "even if we end up having some money, let's never forget how much fun this is. Let's not let that happen to us."

"Hmmm," he said.

"Larry, I'm serious. Remind me, please, if I forget."

Forty years later and I'd pay almost any amount *not* to have to eat tuna out of a can or wait in line with fifty others to use the only bathroom.

How did I let this betrayal happen? The same way it happened that I can't close my jeans, that I meant to join the Peace Corps, that I swore I would never sound like my mother, sell out to the establishment, hold a conservative opinion, or take a job just for money. It took forty years to move from poorer to richer, from canned tuna to Chilean sea bass *en croûte*. We conceived our first son that summer in a tent on the Lido during a hurricane. Now I want a bed. I want indoors. I want water pressure.

Larry, by the way, doesn't exactly have to be dragged kicking and screaming to the reception desk at a nice hotel either, although if it weren't for my corrupting bourgeois influence, he might still be camping.

The seeds of corruption, I fear, were always in me. How else to interpret a letter I wrote to my parents from the kibbutz? I found it recently while sorting through papers in their attic. Even forty years later, I'm embarrassed by my smarmy bid for an infusion of funds.

I start with a diversionary tactic, telling them that we are having a wonderful time at the kibbutz. I let them know that we traveled deck-class on the way over from Piraeus, but that at the kibbutz we have the temporary use of a cabin that contains a chair and a single cot. Then I mention that the guy who normally lives here is away for the month, fulfilling his military requirement, and that unfortunately he has chained his favorite possession, his bike, to the bed, so that every night it's the three of us in the cot. It's harder on Larry than it is on me, I allow, since he gallantly insists upon being next to the bike.

I tell them that the business of the kibbutz is fish farming and that Larry gets up every morning at 4:00 A.M. to drag nets and harvest fish with the other men. They quit at noon because it gets too hot (110 degrees) to work. It's at least as hot in the kitchen, where I pluck chickens from 9:00 A.M. to 4:00 P.M. And by the way, I mention, in a doozy of a postscript, "I might be pregnant." (In fact I was.)

Not surprisingly, a check for one hundred dollars arrived from my parents, and with it a moral dilemma. Since we were living in a commune, where nothing was privately owned, we were supposed to turn the money over to the common treasury. We didn't. Even though we sang the theme from *Exodus* ("This land is mine, God gave this land to me") every morning as we strode to work, we kept quiet about the check.

The fact that we continue to sell out does not mean that we are no longer committed to authenticity; it's the poverty part we're not fond of. Now the challenge is to have authentic experiences in spite of being encumbered by funds.

I find I'm up to the challenge. Occasionally I enjoy staying in castles, a habit I perfected during our *Relais and Chateâux* period in the eighties. I like the rich, heavy tapestries and the way the worn stone steps speak to me of the tread of thousands of feet over dozens of centuries. There's something grand about carrying around a room key the size and weight of an anvil. And what could be more authentic than to sleep under a coat of arms on a bed made for a Medici?

Larry's not impressed. Did I notice the sound and light equipment? Didn't I have an authenticity problem with the Jacuzzi? Does it bother me that they're playing *An American in Paris* on the sound system in the dining room or that the Medici mattress is a Sealy Posturepedic? And by the way, he wonders, have I seen the bill?

Authenticity at any price is elusive. Travelers are doomed to run afoul of Werner Heisenberg's killjoy uncertainty principle. For instance, does posing with a New Guinean wood carver in native dress right after he has taken an imprint of your credit card qualify as legit? Surely it's more authentic than if we stayed home and watched New Guinea on the Travel Channel.

Was our three-day trek in Nepal any less genuine because the Sherpa we hired brought along a toilet tent and two chickens and we were gone for only three days? We walked uphill, didn't we? In Nepal, right? Isn't that trekking? Does somebody have to get lost, or starve?

Authenticity is not what it used to be. In Ulaanbaatar, the capital of Mongolia, they eat tartar sauce and drink Genghis Kahn beer. Sri Lanka, which used to be Ceylon, has a Pizza Hut. Even banana republics have Banana Republics. Our friend Carole was in Lapland, wrapped in reindeer robes, roasting meat on a stick over an open fire when she heard the ring of a fax machine.

Cultural legitimacy, *National Geographic* variety, is hard to find. In 1998 some friends of ours came close. They were part of an exclusive tour group that visited the Asmat tribe in Irian Jaya, Indonesia's most remote province, where polygamy is the norm, bare breasts and penis gourds are the fashion, and people live in grass huts and use Stone Age tools and weapons.

Asmats have a special way of welcoming strangers. In Irian Jaya a simple handshake will not do. Nothing less than a literal reenactment of childbirth will suffice to make a visitor feel at home. Our friends were invited to crawl between their hostess's legs and then suckle briefly at her breasts. They speak about this experience with deep reverence.

When traveling, we find it is possible to create conditions under which authenticity is likely to occur. Westminster Abbey, for instance, is not such a place. What we seek when we travel is that wonderful feeling of being "let in," of no longer being tourists on the outside, with our noses pressed against the pane. We want some kind stranger to come to the door and let us in. We travel for those moments. They make us feel at home.

When in London, for instance, Larry likes to go to a pub and get himself invited to play darts. Once he's had his back slapped by a beery Englishman, he's in. Then he gets more in. He usually leaves the pub smoking an English cigarette, speaking with a cockney accent, and suffused with a desire to buy a tweed cap.

Before I can feel at home in France, I have to go on a picnic. This is preceded by a trip to an outdoor market to purchase the ingredients. Once there, in the interests of authenticity, I must at least attempt to speak French. This works very well for the bread *(du pain)* and the wine *(du vin)*. But when I order *brie,* I launch a shouting match. The proprietor thinks I'm asking for *bruit,* noise.

"*Bruit?*"

"*Non, brie!*"

"*Bruit!!*"

"*Non, brie!!*"

And so forth. Soon everyone in the store is making fun of the American woman who wants to eat bread and noise. My authentic French experience is nicely under way.

Larry and I settle ourselves down on a grassy bank beside a babbling (in French) brook near the Pont du Gard. Quite nearby, a young French couple, their little French toddler, and their French dog are also planning to enjoy a French *pique-nique.*

The French father throws a stick to the dog. The dog leaps into the air and then runs to fetch it. The dog brings it back. The next time the man throws the stick, the dog fetches it and drops it at Larry's feet. We introduce ourselves. He is Claude. He's a farmer. Marie teaches school. The baby is Lisette. Within minutes we are sharing picnics and attempting conversation. They want to know if we'd like to join them tomorrow for Lisette's christening. A real French christening with real French people, in France! We accept. Marie likes my haircut. Besides, Claude and Marie can't see anything wrong with the way I say *brie*. Larry trades Claude a pack of unfiltered Camels for a pack of his unfiltered Gauloises. Lisette launches herself across the grass to my outstretched arms, settles on my lap, and falls asleep. We're in.

Poverty, especially in one's choice of sleeping accommodations, offers the richest opportunities to pierce the tourist veil. During our *Europe on Five Dollars a Day* years we spent an extremely authentic evening in a hotel in Tours. We had to walk up three flights of stairs in order to get to our room. (A sign on the elevator read NE MARCHE PAS.) At is turned out, our sleep was constantly interrupted that night by the sound of staccato heels and work boots climbing up and down the stairs. By about five in the morning we figured it out: we were trying to sleep in a whorehouse. Meanwhile we looked forward to a warm shower and a night's sleep.

LA DOUCHE NE MARCHE PAS, read a sign in the same hand on a note attached to the shower. The sign invited us to use the public baths in the center of town.

"This may be more authenticity than I bargained for," I remember thinking as I sat naked on a long, slatted wooden bench, waiting with a lot of other naked women, who were also getting stripe marks on their buttocks. A matron carrying a stack of frayed towels escorted us to the shower room. There, standing in full view of one another and the matron, we were allowed one pull to get wet, one minute to soap up, and another pull to rinse off.

DÉFENSE DE SIFLER ET CHANTER (No whistling or singing), read a huge sign on the concrete wall. As if.

(If you're the sort of person who insists upon having a wonderful time while you're on vacation, authenticity may not be your thing.)

Doing Nothing

In contrast to our madcap honeymoon, which was marked by eccentric adventures, our first decade of married life was an exercise in stunning conformity.

We got married in our twenties because that's when everybody else was getting married. Then we had two children right away because everybody else was doing that. We even moved to the suburbs because that's where everybody else was moving.

In short, with a few extra dollars in our pockets and two children in diapers, we abandoned our youthful ideals and joined the middle class and the ranks of those whose heads would be displayed on pikes in the event of a revolution.

In February, when everybody else went to the Caribbean for a week, we did too. When they got back, they said they had had a wonderful time. We said we had too.

They went because they needed a rest and wanted to go to an island paradise, relax in the sun, and have someone cater to their every whim.

We didn't have any whims and we didn't believe in paradise, not even as an afterlife experience. Nor did we think we needed to lie down for a week. Nevertheless, we went. We didn't have minds of our own at the time.

Which paradise should we choose? Anguilla, Angilla, Angola, Angora, Attila, Ayatollah, Antilles, Lesser Antilles, Greater Aunt Tilly, Petite Aunt Tilly, Barbados, Barbuda, Big Barbuda, Baby Barbuda, Barbarola, Barbarossa, Barbasol, Barabas? It was confusing.

Some of these islands were half-French and half-Dutch, or half-English and half-Rockefeller, or half–Club Med and half-Hilton. To get to some of them you had to take a big plane, then a little plane, then a little boat, and then a rusty taxi. To get to others you had to take two big planes and one little plane and then one motorboat, one rowboat, and a dugout canoe. At some of them you turned in all your money for a necklace of wooden beads. At others you just turned in all your money. The basic idea was to be carefree.

The first day was usually taken up with the wonder of it all: suddenly it was summer, warm instead of cold, green instead of gray, and the children weren't with us. Best of all, there were always plenty of orientation activities on the first day: the welcoming complimentary tropical drink with plastic monkey, registration, bungalow finding, room showing, tipping, chaise dragging, towel renting, and salamander appreciation.

Day two was always a sobering experience. We would learn for the first, second, or third season in a row that we could not read on the beach. It was just too hot to concentrate. Too hot even for Jackie Collins.

And so, like two amphibious creatures in a PBS

nature documentary, we would lie in the sand until some internal signal as old as life itself would tell us that we had preheated to 350 and it was time to make our way to the sea. There, we would submerge and swim about for several minutes before retracing our steps up the beach to resume our patient vigil on the sand. After a preordained period of time, the amazing cycle of nature would begin again, and back we'd go to the sea. And we'd do all this without ever laying eggs.

We became so bored that Larry began to look forward to dinner even though it was the same menu every night — local fish with a hibiscus blossom, pureed taro root with a hibiscus blossom, and a hollowed-out pineapple filled with tropical fruit.

My major daytime activity (besides watching the sweat pool in my belly button) was getting a tan. This was before anybody had ever heard about global warming or the ozone layer. This was when *melanoma* sounded like an imported fruit. Getting a tan was pretty much the whole point of going to the Caribbean. It was something to bring home with

you in midwinter, something to make other Caucasians who didn't have one feel conspicuously pale.

Getting a tan was serious work, a complex and delicately nuanced procedure. Where should I lie down? What should I lie down on? A towel? A chaise? Where to position it vis-à-vis the sun? Should I use my reflector? How much iodine should I put in how much baby oil? Then, after the carefully choreographed application of the oil, came the time to turn to Larry and say those five little words without which no meaningful tanning could occur: "Will you do my back?" It was important not to have strap marks—everybody knew that. But only a very few knew to tip their head backward from time to time to allow the sun to tan that place at the top of the neck that is usually shaded by the chin.

Typically, by the third day, Larry would alternate pacing the beach with demonstrating to other people's children how to build drip castles. By day four he resumed smoking. Now each time he lit up, I had my choice of two new activities — looking daggers or hurling invectives.

Usually, as we neared the end of our stay, I had projected my fury onto the steel band, who would not stop playing "Yellow Bird" although I had sent them many anonymous notes, which at least gave me something to do.

On the final day we often found ourselves wondering if it is true that if you tear the tails off salamanders, they will grow back.

Amazingly, it took us three such vacations before we realized that we didn't like the Caribbean.

What we didn't understand then that we do understand now is that Larry and I don't go on vacation to relax. Vacations are for work. We'll have plenty of time to rest when we get home.

We do stop for beauty, but we don't always think the same things are beautiful. For instance, I don't particularly like sunsets, especially Caribbean sunsets with palm trees. Even when I'm

right there, sitting on the beach, virtual reality intrudes: I see the photo on the wish-you-were-here postcard or the calendar from our insurance company. For many summers, just to keep him company, I'd sit with Larry on the beach on Cape Cod, staring at the horizon, watching the red blob of the sun pass behind dark, messy shreds of clouds and disappear very, very slowly into the ocean. All the while—for at least twenty minutes—Larry is making appreciative moaning and gasping noises.

"Isn't it beautiful!" he says, forgetting he's with me.

"If you saw that in your sink," I say, "you'd reach for the Comet."

We don't like to unwind. There's nothing Zen about us. It's not unusual to come upon Larry relaxing at home on a Sunday afternoon, working a crossword puzzle, vacuuming the rugs, and washing the dishes. I can talk on the phone, answer my E-mail, and moisturize without feeling the least bit stressed. People who like us think of us as energetic and productive. People who don't, think we're workaholic freaks who won't last much longer. The point is, a transatlantic cruise would not be a good vacation choice for us, unless our ship came under enemy attack or ran into the perfect storm.

Since the Caribbean years, we have made a conscious effort to avoid do-nothing vacations. Occasionally, though, as a result of careless planning or bad luck, we find ourselves with nothing to do. For instance, in the spring of 1993 we got stuck in Paris during Pentecost, a holiday weekend so holy that it lasts for four days and everything is *fermé*, including museums, concert halls, and most of the restaurants. We were frantic. We sat in the Tuileries, glared at the flowers, and entertained anti-Pentecostal thoughts. When we got tired of that, we roamed the streets, seeking entrance to something, anything. On one of our many such excursions we found an open *pharmacie*. We roamed the aisles pretending the place was the Louvre. We examined the items appreciatively, as if every L'Oréal were a Leonardo, every toothpaste a Tintoretto, and every shampoo-conditioner a Toulouse-Lautrec. Hungry for more, Larry the art lover went off to Notre-Dame to count the gargoyles. I made a desperate purchase, went back to the hotel, and dyed my hair champagne blond. It was something to do.

During a trip to Turkey, a daylong rainstorm brought me to such a frenzy of inactivity that I abandoned my career as a freelance writer and became a rug merchant.

We were in Kalkan, a village on the Mediterranean that sounds like dog food but is otherwise very attractive. We had the car packed and were about to drive east toward Antalya when it began to rain and with such force that we ducked into the nearest shop—not surprisingly a rug store—to seek cover.

The rain did not let up for hours. For a while we admired the kilims. The owner (an engaging woman named Henrietta) unfurled one rug after another for our admiration. When there seemed to be nothing left to do, we bought a small kilim. It continued to pour. By the time the rain finally abated, I was the store owner's United States rug rep.

My friends at home were enormously supportive.

When the first kilim shipment arrived in its burlap shroud, they showed up in my driveway, their checkbooks in hand. I went out of business six months later, when my friends ran out of floor space.

Sometimes we fall off the wagon and try to relax. We kid ourselves into believing we can do it—just this once—and get away with it. Why else would we have signed up for a weeklong barge trip through the waterways of Burgundy? Is there anything more confining, sedentary, slow, and tranquil than a barge trip?

We had a fabulous time for the first few minutes. The scenery along the gently winding canal was reminiscent of my childhood picture books—rows of poplar trees, tiny stone villages, castles, grazing cows, jumping fish, rolling hills, and patchwork-quilted fields. It was heavenly. I'm not sure about Larry, but I think I relaxed, if you can be relaxed at the same time that you're saying, "Wow, I'm so relaxed."

Within hours, the miles and miles of relentless, uninterrupted tranquillity and nonstop loveliness started getting on our nerves. An occasional fisherman standing on the bank, a quaint straw hat on his head, an old-fashioned bamboo pole in hand, might have broken the monotony were it not for the tedious local custom of waving, which obliged us to wave back—from the moment we drifted into view until the moment we passed out of sight. According to Larry's calculations the barge was moving at two and a half miles per hour.

"The frail elderly can move faster on walkers," he said as we waved and paced the deck while grinding our molars down to the gum line.

The next day, Larry paid a visit to the captain to explain our predicament: we were professional athletes whose muscles would atrophy if we were not allowed to jog in place on the deck for at least an hour each day.

He got the captain's permission, but it was rescinded almost immediately when the other forty-eight passengers, now blissfully relaxed, complained that the pounding and panting were threatening their peace and were not what they had in mind when they signed up for a barge cruise.

Undeterred, Larry the mediator went to the captain with another proposal: we would get off the barge whenever it stopped to go through a lock. Then we'd run alongside the barge on the towpath and get back on board at the next lock.

It was *"pas normal,"* the captain said, but he agreed.

Since we ran more than twice as fast as the barge drifted, we kept passing it. Even though we waved every time we went by, the formerly relaxed voyagers found us unnerving and were now talking about wanting their money back.

If it weren't for the bikes stowed on board, intended for passenger use when the barge made the occasional stop in a town, we would have had to jump ship.

Larry made what was to be his final visit to the captain. Would he let us get off with the bikes every morning after breakfast and then meet us at a designated place and allow us to reembark every evening in time for dinner?

It's *"pas normal,"* Larry added conspiratorially, but so what? We wouldn't tell if he wouldn't. We would not bike back and forth on the towpath in view of the barge. We would immediately venture into nearby towns and visit tourist sites. We would be gone all day. We wouldn't be seen or heard from until dinnertime. The captain jumped at the chance.

Larry misses his work when he goes on vacation. He calls it up whenever he gets a chance. How are his divorces and his zoning hearings? Have any decisions come down? Have any checks come in? He's more likely to call when we're vacationing in the United States. When we're abroad, he feels so far away that it's easier on him emotionally to make a clean break. This makes him particularly vulnerable to the siren call of international advocacy, even though people who live in foreign countries live under legal systems that do not resemble our own. Nor does he let the fact that he is not licensed to practice law in any other country discourage him.

In the fall of 2000, we stayed in a friend's authentic thatch-roofed cottage in the tiny village of Kinvara on Galway Bay. After three extremely quaint days, we reached our tolerance for inner peace and outer rain and were ready for some utter chaos. It came just in time, in the form of a land dispute that Larry learned about while hanging out in the local pub.

Contractors from the big city were threatening to build a residential development of twenty-three tract homes in this village of 342 souls, eleven pubs, and one broken-down castle, where nothing has changed in fifty years, where plumbing pipes run down the outside of buildings, where cows pasture by the side of the roads as if they thought they were in India, and where nobody's even heard of Lycra or hand weights.

The villagers wanted to fight back. Larry let it slip at the pub that night that he was a lawyer with a specialty in land use. He volunteered to help them.

One of Larry's more sober potential clients, speaking for the others, questioned the relevance of American to Irish zoning laws, but Larry patiently allayed their fears by explaining that they deviated in only the smallest details. Of course, if they actually had to go to court, they would need to hire an

Irish lawyer, but essentially the issues were the same: Would the increased traffic adversely affect the cows? Would the proposed houses interfere with the neighbors' view of the castle? Larry assured them he dealt with such routine matters all the time in Westport, Connecticut.

The papers had to be filed in three days. There was no time for delay. For the balance of our stay the neighbors gathered in our living room on a daily basis to plot and plan against the wily city folk. The builder's plans were permanently unfurled on the kitchen table, surrounded by Padraic McKinney, Connor Joyce, Prather Houlihan, Kathleen Donovan, and Larry O'Lawyer. Larry was no longer doing nothing. Neither was I—I was a barmaid, serving pints of Guinness. We were on vacation. There was work to be done.

The Modified Marital Plan

Multiple-couple travel tends to occur about five or ten years after the honeymoon, when bride and groom are pretty much done plumbing one another's depths, and wonder is reduced to what's for dinner. (My Aunt Lily did take her psychiatrist on her honeymoon, but the circumstances were extraordinary. It was her fifth marriage.)

In no way should the desire to invite another couple on vacation be taken as an indictment of the marriage; rather, it represents the inevitable, if sober, triumph of reality over the eternal, if heartbreaking, appeal of the romantic myth. We all have to grow up. Marriage loves company. Who has not seen or been part of a couple dining together at a restaurant in total silence, but has anyone seen two couples at the same table, utterly mute from soup to nuts?

Traveling with another couple is a lot like being married to them, so it is important to make a suitable choice. Liking them is, of course, fundamental, but it's not enough. They have to like each other. Larry and I once went on a sailing vacation in the Greek islands with a couple from California who, unbeknownst to us, did not. This became clear on day three while we were moored near the sacred island of Delos. Henry, always a bit of a cutup, applied low-fat salad dressing all over his body instead of tanning lotion, causing his wife, Adele, to call him "totally disgusting." (The little bits of pimiento clinging to his chest hairs *were* unappetizing.) In retaliation, Henry set himself adrift in the lifeboat, and Adele locked herself in the only bathroom on the thirty-two-foot boat. Larry took Henry's side. I took Adele's. One week later, Henry and Adele filed for divorce. We were almost next.

Nor can you be sure that you will enjoy vacationing together even if you like them and they do like each other. Some irritating vacation behaviors cannot be predicted, no matter how hard you try. "Will you feel compelled to comment on my calorie intake each morning?" is not a question most people would think to ask a prospective traveling companion. Nor do you necessarily think to ask if your travel companions have to find a local gym so they can do their full workout each day. And how could you possibly know that she will betray you by taking twice as much luggage to Mexico as she said she would, or that he would summon the waiter with *"El checko, por favor"*?

On the other hand, there are a number of predictable areas of concern that can be inquired about in advance, which is why savvy traveling couples negotiate prenuptial and separation agreements before plighting their traveling troths.

Assuming you've agreed upon a destination, a discussion of accommodations is the obvious place to begin. It is a good way to determine whether your prospective traveling companions think that a vacation is a time to spend liberally or be cheap, without confronting the issue of money directly. For instance, the time has long since passed when Larry and I found it amusing to share a bathroom at the end of the hall, even with friends. We have enough trouble sharing one with each other. Failure to achieve consensus on so important a matter as a three-star château versus a no-star yurt should be taken as an indication of terminal incompatibility.

It's important to pay close attention and ask questions. When Larry and I were planning a vacation in Japan with our friends Carole and Alan, I failed to pick up on Carole's expressed desire to spend at least one night in a traditional Japanese *ryokan*. If I had said, "What's that like?" Carole might have told me that it involves living in a paper room and sleeping on the floor on a very large place mat with your head resting on a pillow stuffed with Rice Krispies. Since I didn't ask, I have to take responsibility for a night of traditional Japanese insomnia. However, I still hold her responsible for failing to tell me that in order to use the bathroom, you must hang from a rope and, when finished, pull on a chain and then swing out of the bathroom like a Flying Wallenda or be inundated by a tsunami of a flush. Nor did she mention that they served pickled eggs for breakfast.

As in marriage, separation is often the key to happiness, since travel styles differ from couple to couple. This is not a problem if you know about these differences in advance and make appropriate adjustments. There are hundreds of Greek ruins on the Aegean coast between Istanbul and Izmir, many of them on hilltops. Our friend Monica has to visit and climb on top of all of them, including Troy, which even *her* guidebook described as "a few vague piles of stone." Larry and I, on the other hand, are quite content to knock off the requisite sites — one theater, one temple to Aphrodite, one temple to Apollo, one gymnasium, and two agoras — and then take a short amble in a field of poppies, followed by a little sit-down and a bottle of wine.

Some people like to see countries. Others prefer to ingest them. People who want to see all the sights tend to skip lunch, relinquishing the dolmas, eggplant, and baklava that for another couple, one like us, might justify the entire trip. We were completely forthcoming about our slovenly cultural ways and our affection for eating lunch while seated, as were

Monica and her husband, Doug, about their need to see it all. Because of our mutual candor, we were able to agree in advance to a marriage of convenience. We would rent two cars, split up after breakfast, and remarry at dinner.

Museum visitations are often a sticking point for which a brief separation is a mutually satisfying solution. "Do you rent the headphones?" is a good way of distinguishing a serious art lover from someone who looks at the van Goghs and then heads for the museum shop to buy *The Starry Night* in a mailing tube.

When you're traveling with another couple, the numbers can work for or against you. You have two more people to walk and talk with, two more people to share the driving, and one other person who's interested in going shopping. On the other hand, you also have two more people to wait for in the lobby and two more people to complain about their jet lag. Now that you are four, it is also twice as likely that someone will lose a passport or leave their prescription drugs in the last hotel. However, it is also twice as likely that no one will yell at you. This is because the other couple is watching.

When two marriages travel together, they tend to

be on their best behavior. A kind of benign competition for best marriage takes place as each couple
tries to display its union in the most favorable light.
The rain in Spain stayed mainly wherever we went,
at least for the ten days we vacationed there with
our friends Karen and Barry. Had either couple
been traveling alone, I suspect the mood would
have descended rapidly through the first four of
Elisabeth Kübler-Ross's five stages of grief—denial,
anger, bargaining, and depression—without ever
arriving at acceptance. However, because of the
alchemy of our foursome, we were practically singing
in the rain. On the eighth consecutive day of precipitation, we ducked into a restaurant, any restaurant,
to escape what was a torrential gale, the kind that
turns umbrellas inside out. After lunch, the rain had
diminished to a steady downpour, causing Barry to
remark, "Aren't we lucky?" Had I been married to
him and had we been traveling alone and had he
made such a comment, I would have torn his head
off. As it was, no one dared be grumpy in the face of

his pathological good cheer. What might have been a faux pas de deux turned into esprit de corps.

On another occasion, while having lunch together on the Ramblas in Barcelona, Larry detected what he thought was hostility in my voice. (I think I said something like, "Do you think you're really going to be able to eat all those tapas?") "Hostile? I'm not being hostile," I said. "It's not what you're saying, it's your tone," he answered. "Tone? What tone?" I replied, looking to Karen for support. "I'm not touching that one," she answered, and we all enjoyed a good, knowing, intermarital laugh.

Packing

Packing is the original sin of travel. In the beginning there was no packing. There weren't even any clothes. If Adam and Eve had not gotten themselves banished from the Garden of Eden, their children and their children's children would not have to decide between taking one pair of underwear and rinsing it out every night, or packing several, thereby taking up space that might better be used for a wide-spectrum antibiotic, a current adapter, or an alternate pair of walking shoes. We would all still be naked in Paradise. There wouldn't be any need to get away from it all. As it is, in our fallen state, we must travel endlessly throughout the world collecting frequent-flier points, doomed never to know if we've packed the right stuff.

Having nothing to wear is a condition I take with me wherever I go, no matter how many and various the items of clothing I possess. I take them out and I put them back. I lay out. I try on. I accessorize. I fold. I roll. I assess all the bottled items I'm planning to bring with me for their explosive potential, especially the hand lotion and shampoo, and decide to isolate them in a Ziploc bag. I count the days I will be away in pills and deposit them in my Sunday-through-Saturday plastic case. I pack them. Then I unpack them and put them in my purse, in case of luggage loss. Then I dump everything out and change suitcases. Invariably while packing I feel the need to shop. I dash from store to store in a sweat, like a druggie in need of a fix, at once ashamed and determined.

For extra credit I worry about what to wear on the plane. Jeans are getting too tight. I gave them up in a lavatory over Tokyo in 1992 when I discovered grommet indentations on my belly. It was during that same flight that I invented an inflatable out-fit for air travelers, inspired by astronauts' space suits. It's an all-purpose, self-regulating minienvi-ronment, equipped with gourmet food, music, TV, and movies. The pod is made out of opaque, flexible plastic so that you can lounge nude inside. It's even got its own waste disposal and air recirculation sys-tem that guarantees that the only cold you catch will be your own. Plus it has exterior handles in case someone needs to move you into the aisle, and in the event of an emergency landing, you can serve as your own flotation device. Until I get the patent and enough investors to make a prototype, I settle for a sweat suit and sneakers so that all of me can swell with impunity.

My friend Brett has an irrational fear of wrinkles. Before she packs, she sends the clothes she's plan-ning to take with her to be dry-cleaned, whether they need it or not, just so they come back wrapped in plastic. Then she places them in a suitcase so large that she doesn't have to fold anything.

Another friend, Lucie, has worse problems. She

never has the right luggage. She wanders through stores trying out suitcases as if she were tasting porridge. Should she get the one that the gorilla jumps on in the commercials and can't break, or maybe go with something less flamboyant and more patriotic, like American Tourister?

No matter how much I learn in advance about my destination's climate, topography, style of dress, midday highs, and evening lows, not to mention its average monthly precipitation, I seem not to be able to process the information to any useful effect. Is hot in Paris the same as hot in Connecticut? I cannot imagine. Should I take an umbrella? It rained 2.1 inches in Prague last August, but was that all at once, or a little bit nearly every day? I wouldn't know what to pack for a vacation in a nudist colony. I'd get hung up worrying about a suitable traveling outfit: Sweats? A muu-muu? My imagination fails me. (I have a similar problem with travel books. No matter how intently I read them before a trip, no matter how informative, well-written, and sometimes even interesting they may be, I still don't know what I want to see or how long I want to stay until I get there.) I compensate for not knowing what to take by taking everything I own. I'm one of the vacationing homeless. I pull my worldly possessions in a suitcase on a leash behind me.

It is as if I believe I must take everything I own because no matter where I'm going — Paris or Peru — they don't have it. Larry has tried his best, including the use of both reason and sarcasm, to reassure me, but to no avail.

"My sun hat! I forgot my sun hat!" I cry as we run to the gate at La Guardia.

"I would hazard a guess," says Larry, "that they have sun hats in Jamaica."

Someplace in my brain where I'm sane, I must know that I'll be able to find a sun hat in Jamaica or a toothbrush in Paris. Jacques Chirac, after all, must brush his teeth. He probably even flosses. But I am not soothed. Will I find tweezers in Dublin? It rains a lot in Ireland, but do they pluck? My fears defy reason. I am sure that nothing I have forgotten is available in any other country in the world.

It may be that packing is particularly difficult for me because my earliest ideas of what packing should be came from the films of the forties, where stars like Anne Baxter or Loretta Young made it look too easy. They grabbed armloads of dresses from their closets, sometimes with the hangers still attached, folded them hastily into their suitcases, and then struggled to close the lid and snap it shut. Usually something chiffon was hanging out as our heroine, dressed in a cloth coat, picked up her bag and closed the door behind her. Then she would show up in a New York hotel room with a fully accessorized wardrobe of gowns, gabardine suits, peignoir sets, a riding habit, and a change of fur coats.

I wish I could be fancy-free like my friend Mirela. On a recent trip to India she packed clothes she no longer enjoyed wearing and then, like an ambassador from Goodwill, left them, outfit after outfit, in hotel rooms from Delhi to Bombay. Why can't I be cool like those postmodernist hippies who fill one half of a backpack with a change of clothing and the other half with bottled springwater? Or, failing that, I would settle for being the kind of savvy woman who packs five mix-and-match separates in black and beige tones, made of uncrushable fabric that breathes, plus a colorful scarf she knows how to tie eight ways. But I am not. I am an out-of-control packer. Larry is too. We are each other's enablers. What else does "made for each other" mean?

Whenever we're faced with two empty suitcases, we try to keep each other under control. We take it one outfit at a time. "Are you bringing khakis?" I ask Larry, who is fighting his own packing demons on his side of the bed. He is. I am reassured. I'll take mine.

"How about three T-shirts?" he suggests, keeping the numbers down to what he knows he can handle. "Sounds about right," I agree. He in turn wants to know if I think he can get away with one sport jacket and one pair of decent trousers, in case we do anything slightly fancy in the evening. "Absolutely.

And I'll take one pair of black slacks and a blouse," I offer.

So far so good. These are our finest marital packing moments. We are centered. We are open and honest. We are mutually supportive. We are fighting a common enemy and working together toward a common goal—fitting everything into carry-on so we never have to go to baggage claim.

I'm always the one to give in to temptation first, a precedent established by Eve in Genesis 3. Just when we're virtually finished and all that we have left to put in are the toiletries, I am seized by a perverse and irresistible urge to pack more. I know I'm engaging in destructive behavior. I even know I'm going to be sorry. But I don't care.

"Sweetheart," I say, "wouldn't you like to have another outfit, just in case?"

He bites. What began as a commitment to control our packing habit ends in betrayal and a race to the bottom. He slips in an extra jacket. I retaliate with a sweater. He ups the ante with two more pairs of slacks. I pack three. We take a quick time-out while

we head to the attic for larger suitcases. I end by
packing a dress I don't even wear when I'm at home.
He stuffs in a pair of black wing tips. I tuck in some
heels. We are like two bulimics with spoons in front
of an open fridge. It's Paradise Lost all over again.
No wonder Adam and Eve were sent packing.

Shopping

No matter what clothes I ultimately decide to take with me, when I get to my destination I invariably need to go shopping. Not *need* in the sense of "I *need* to cover my body with an animal skin because I am a Cro-Magnon woman in prehistoric times and it's cold outside," but *need* in the sense of "I haven't a thing to wear."

When I'm seized by such a compulsion, Larry usually refuses to go with me. I try to sell him on the idea that shopping expeditions are legitimate sightseeing events and that he should think of the stores as minimuseums where one can purchase the exhibits, and the conversations with salespeople as rare and spontaneous opportunities for cultural exchange, but he's not buying. Madrid is famous for leather, so I have to buy boots; Ireland is full of sheep, so I must visit sweaters; and a kimono tour is compulsory in Japan. Paris is where all shopping hell breaks loose.

I was there in the spring of 1986, mostly on vacation with Larry, and partly to report on the International Sommelier's award banquet at the Abbaye de Royaumont for an American travel magazine. I didn't learn until we got to Paris that the event was formal. No "black tie optional." When wine is involved, the French don't kid around. It would be a four-fork affair with more gold braid, medals, ribbons, drummers, heel clicking, and smart turns than Veterans Day at Arlington National Cemetery.

We were staying with friends. Luckily our host had a tux and was about Larry's size. Our hostess had a formal gown, but *—grâce à Dieu—* she was not my size. It was a dream come true: I was in Paris and I actually *needed* to go shopping.

In view of the degree of difficulty of this particular

couture assignment, Larry decides he'd better come with me. He knows that if left to my own devices I will hold back and try to save money. He wants to be there to remind me that this is a special occasion and that I should splurge and buy myself something really wonderful. He is right. I have already decided that I must first try a discount shop. (Part of needing to shop is needing a bargain. It cancels out the guilt.)

"But it's a *formal*. I'm only going to wear it once," I protest.

"This is a once-in-a-lifetime event," he says, turning my words against me.

He also reminds me that most women would kill to be married to a man like him, who encourages his wife to spend money on clothes, and perhaps I should have my head examined.

Meanwhile, I pull on jeans and sneakers and throw my traveler's checks into my pocketbook in case they don't take *plastique*. I hope that I can remember enough French to buy a dress—if the word for *dress* is *robe*, what's *evening dress, robe de soir?* Or *du soir?* What if that means bathrobe? I seem determined to drive myself and him crazy, even before I set out. Larry makes his usual skewed attempt to reassure me. "In a world of clothes, hangers, price tags, and sales-women," he says, "I have every confidence that you will find a way to make yourself understood."

We step out into the street. I mean to rush by the corner pastry shop without looking, but before I can help myself, I have established eye contact with a pear tart. Larry gives me that old come-hither look, and we fall into line at the counter. I estimate how many times I'll have to jog around the park the next day to exact my pound of flesh. It occurs to me that I have been in Paris for almost a week and I have not heard anyone say *calories,* or *cholesterol,* or even *arterial plaque.* The French do not season their food with regret. Even so, I don't buy the tart; Larry does. I eat half of his.

When I walk in Paris, I study the women as they stroll toward me. Usually they stare brazenly back at me. Neither of us blinks. We lock eyes until we either must stop and meet face-to-face, or pass out of one another's view forever. In those few seconds of contact, each conducts a body search. We probe for one another's secrets. We quickly slip in and out of one another's skin. We learn what we can. When Larry does what I'm doing, it's called being on the make. When I do it, it's called testing the competition. I have consummated at least fifty such encounters before I get to my destination. The results of my womanizing are, as usual, inconclusive. I am no closer to identifying that certain je ne sais quoi that French women seem to have.

Once in the store, I shed my clothes and try to find a hook on the wall, which is the best way to stake a claim at Mendes. Mendes is the Parisian answer to Loehmann's, except that at Mendes, clothing by Yves Saint Laurent and Lanvin is routine, whereas at Loehmann's you're euphoric if you find a Calvin Klein that hasn't had its label removed.

"Be sure to come out and show them to me!" are Larry's parting words as I disappear into a warehouse-size changing room.

I head for the nearest rack. Another woman ar-

rives and begins to look through the dresses alongside me. I size her up through narrowing, gimlet
eyes. She's a ten on top; a twelve, maybe a fourteen,
on the bottom. She has a high, bony chicken chest.
She is thick of waist, heavy of upper arm, and broad
of beam. I, on the other hand, am a nicely propor-
tioned size eight, and starving.

Etched on both our faces are enough laugh lines
to indicate that we have been amused for at least four
decades. Her blond hair falls lank to her shoulders,
emphasizing, it seems to me, the first signs of jowls.
Recently I have had my red hair cut short. I brush
it upward, away from my face, to give me what the
guy who cuts my hair calls "a lift."

In the face department, maybe we're a draw.
When it comes to bodies, it's no contest. So how
come she's trying on a violet taffeta Yves Saint Laurent that's at least a size too small for her, which
plunges directly and precipitously to the waist — the
same dress I just rejected a moment ago as gorgeous, but too flamboyant, too expensive, and too
young for me? Plus I don't deserve it. (Some part of

me that does not wish me well is hell-bent on making what could be a genuine spree into a joyless exercise in self-loathing.)

None of this bothers Ms. France. She doesn't even look at the price. She doesn't pause to ask herself, "Can I throw this in the dryer?" She just slides into it. Her chest rises like a Perdue carcass from the violet décolletage. She steps into her high heels. (This lady doesn't wear Reeboks. She'd sooner have her legs amputated.)

She pirouettes in front of the mirror. The peplum bobbles comically on her huge hips. She places one foot forward at an angle to the other, slides her hands lovingly up her own flanks, rakes her fingers through her hair, tosses back her head, wets her lips, and puts the make on her own reflection in the mirror.

What's she got that I haven't got? I think I know. It is the certain knowledge that she is beautiful. So what if she's wrong? She's happy, isn't she?

Besides, the longer she preens there, exuding a musk of self-esteem more French than Chanel No. 5, the more beautiful she becomes. I, who just moments ago saw every line and bulge, now find myself viewing her through a more generous lens, as if she were backlit and I were filming her through chiffon. I find her conviction that she is beautiful utterly convincing. I am seduced. And I'm not even a consumer.

I've got to have that dress. I wait, smoldering while she decides whether or not she'll take it. I keep my eyes averted, affecting disinterest. After a moment, I feel something change in the air around me. I look up. Ms. France has turned away from the mirror, and we are face-to-face. She is posed in front of me like Venus on the half shell—dewy, expectant. *"L'aimez-vous?"* ("Do you like it?"), she asks.

"Ce n'est pas grand-chose," I reply carelessly, letting her know I think the dress is nothing special. I watch her face flinch, fracture, and craze with hurt. Quickly she turns back to the mirror for what she hopes will be a reassuring look, but instead she begins to tug at the peplum.

Just in case I have aroused her suspicions, I decide to send her the international signal of shopper surrender. I put my clothes back on.

I sling my purse over my shoulder and move resolutely toward the door.

It is just a matter of time. I hide out behind a coatrack, watching while she reaches back, releases the zipper, and slowly steps out of the dress. She puts it back on the hanger and, avoiding the sight of herself in the mirror, leaves the store. The dress is mine.

This time I take off my Reeboks before I put on the dress. I stand on my toes, mimicking the high heels—something gold and strappy—that I'll buy to go with it. I pivot and examine myself in profile.

Perhaps I will let my hair grow long again. Then I could put it up in a careless knot on top of my head, allowing for a few tendrils to hang fetchingly about my ears and the nape of my neck. Maybe I'll grow my nails too.

I flip over the price tag, divide francs into dollars, and come up with an astounding $350, more than I've ever spent for any dress. So what. So what if I only wear it once. I apply some fresh lipstick, brush my hair, and lovingly air-kiss the mirror. I've got to show Larry.

He rises from his seat when he sees me. He takes my hands and holds me at arm's length for a long look and then twirls me around. "Beautiful," he says. "You look beautiful. You are the best-looking woman in Paris. Buy it."

I flip over the tag.

"Are you sure it's not too expensive?"

"Buy it," he says. "I insist."

I am nearly overwhelmed by the sweetness of this man, pitting himself against my intransigent craziness, but not quite.

"Are you sure it's not too plunging, too purple? Are you sure it's not too young for me?" I ask, and nearly wreck the whole thing.

"Buy it," he says, and I do.

His Vacation

Marriage is all about compromise; so is traveling while married. In the honeymoon years, when our blood was hot and the earth moved on a nightly basis, it was easy enough to agree about almost anything. Will I hike up Vesuvius because he wants to? Yes! Will he make a detour through Naples so I can buy the dishes I admired in a New York restaurant? Yes! But now, after so many years of marriage, will I go on a six-day white-water rafting trip on the Colorado River because he thinks it would be fun? "Yes," I said. "Yes I will. Yes."

I had absolutely no hope that I would enjoy this

trip. I don't like to be too cold. I don't like to be too hot. I don't like to be too high. I don't like to be too low. I don't like to be frightened and I don't like to sleep in a bag. It was a compromise. I did it for love.

Larry likes camping. One of the ways I got him to marry me was to pretend I liked it too. But gradually, after we were married, I reverted to indoors and percale. I did a lot of pretending before we were married, but I wasn't the only one. When we were dating, Larry told me that whenever he entered a city for the first time, he was obliged to go to the local police department and register his hands as lethal weapons. So in a way we were even. But I still felt bad about my betrayal.

Larry has been a trial lawyer all his adult life — years spent convincing idealistic wives that amicable divorce is an oxymoron, years spent trying to convince hostile zoning boards that the shelves his clients would like to hang in their living room (for which they need a variance) will not further contribute to the traffic problem on the Post Road. This means decades of needing to be smart, defensive,

aggressive, persuasive, villainous, heroic, perpetually in control, and above all a winner. It can get on
a person's nerves. And here he was, about to celebrate his fiftieth birthday, and I had denied him
nearly a lifetime of camping pleasure. Would it kill
me to pretend I liked camping just one more time?

A quick read of the outfitter's catalog describing
the trip suggested that it might. A number of sentences seemed ominous: sentences like "Breakfast is
served at 5:00 A.M.," or "When you are splashed—
drenched may be a better word—going through the
rapids, you will get very cold," and my favorite, "We
carry out all wastes."

But here and there I found words of encouragement. "We serve wine with some meals," and
"Please let us know if you're having a birthday or
anniversary on the trip." That did it. The idea of
Larry stripped to the waist, a red bandanna tied
around his neck, blowing out candles in the bottom
of the Grand Canyon, was irresistible. He would
love it. I signed the release forms indemnifying the
outfitters for all legal responsibility in the event of

death or maiming, mailed in a deposit, and began to shop for the items on the packing list, none of which were available at Saks. In spite of the fact that I followed the list like a fascist, I could not fit all my stuff into the little black rubber duffel provided by the outfitters. I had to triage one of the two pairs of trousers allowed and the recommended extra pair of sneakers, just to make room for my pharmaceuticals. Even so, I bonfired all my vanities and brought along only those prescription and over-the-counter items necessary to maintain life and other regularities. The night before departure, I bathed, shampooed, conditioned, shaved, moisturized, pared, plucked, and flossed.

On day one, we put into the river at Lees Ferry, where the canyon begins. There, the Colorado is wide and tranquil and the canyon walls are unimposing and gray. In addition to the oarsman, Tony, I spend the first day in a yellow rubber boat with Larry, a bank manager and hot-air balloonist from Allentown, Pennsylvania, named Nancy, and a thirty-something woman named Diane, winsome in a khaki visor hat.

No sooner is the boat in the water than Larry re-
focuses all of his considerable type A talents on con-
trolling this adventure. He ties things down. He
pushes off. He wants to row.

I try a different tack. "How do you get out of here
if you're having a terrible time?" I ask Tony. There
is no way, he tells me, unless you are really disabled,
like your back is broken, or you're dead, in which

case they radio for a rescue helicopter and bill you or your estate $350 an hour. Tony also tells me about two women from a former trip who flounced onto his boat the first day with their husbands and announced that the trip was not their idea. "They were determined to hate every minute of it," says Tony, "and they did." And then he tells about the lady "who came down here all high-strung. In a coupla days she threw away all her tranquilizer pills she was taking." Sitting across from Tony, trussed in a life jacket, swathed in Gore-Tex from head to toe, anticipating my first rapid, I wondered which it would be—the helicopter, the six-day sulk, or born again drug-free?

By day two I know it will not be the helicopter or the six-day sulk. As anticipated, I am scared of the rapids and uncomfortable in a sleeping bag. But as well as I know myself, I have failed to take into account a serious character flaw that is serving me well on this trip. I tend to behave myself when people are watching. If I were alone with Larry, lying in my sleeping bag, and I learned that the birds flying around the night sky were really bats, I might scream or gag or make unreasonable demands about making them go away. With twenty other people watching, I just take a sleeping pill and roll over. Or if I were alone with Larry on a rubber boat, bouncing off boulders, while sheets of icy water invaded my Gore-Tex and streamed down my cleavage, I would not say, "Wow! This is fun!" In other words, I'm a show-off.

Larry, on the other hand, is getting bored and restless. He's seen enough rocks. He's seen enough water. He's been through enough rapids. Now what?

By day three the canyon walls loom red and mauve as the river cuts its way deeper into time, taking us with it. We stop on a white, sandy beach for lunch. We eat our way up and down the food chain, specializing in bacon, peanut butter, and M&M's. It's as if we'd never heard of low fat.

We hike five hundred feet straight up to explore an Anasazi granary. I am very frightened but I behave, although I do most of the trip up and back on all fours. After the climb, I am too hot, too hot not to throw myself into the Colorado River.

Now I am too cold. So cold that my brain throbs. And still I behave. "Hey!" I cajole the others. "C'mon in. It's only cold water." Soon all the women are bathing. Shampoo, razors, and emery boards appear from secret stashes. Diane has dental floss. Then we do the laundry.

By day four the canyon spreads high and wide above us. We read the rocks like clouds. There's a two-headed dog, a nude, a whale, and Winston Churchill. Suspended temporarily in a state of nature with total strangers, people take liberties. They fall in love. They confide. Diane tells Ralph he'd look a lot better without a ponytail. Larry tells Diane that he covets her hat. Diane asks Larry if he thinks it's possible that two people, if they really respect each other and want to be fair, can get divorced amicably. Fred tells me that his wife left him because he would not help her with the household chores. I tell Fred I don't blame her. Bill refuses to be photographed. Lowell tells me that when I get out of my sleeping bag in the morning, I have "jail hair." Larry tells Tony he talks like they do on *Hee Haw!*

On day five the canyon ravels and unravels Escher-like, background moving to foreground, fooling and dazzling the eye. Larry has passed from Larry Lawyer, through bored and restless, through open and honest, and is now drifting into mellow. He no longer ties down. He no longer wants to row. He no longer wants to be a lawyer. Maybe he'll open up a little sandwich shop. And yes, Diane, there is civilized divorce.

We have all changed. We are all relaxed, happy, genial. Fred offers to do my dishes. Diane changes her mind about Ralph's ponytail. I'm so used to behaving myself that I'm actually having a wonderful time. Tony says he's thinking of leading a nine-day white-water rafting trip in Chile next February. He wants to know if anyone's interested. I hear myself say, "I am." The prepercale kid in me has taken over. Although I have not yet thrown away my pharmaceuticals, I am born again.

We celebrate Larry's birthday the last night on

the river. Tomorrow we will hike ten miles up and out of the canyon to what now seems like the unreal world. We don't want to leave. Everybody sings to Larry. He is completely surprised and moved. Tony bakes him a chocolate cake in a Dutch oven. "Hey, pard, remember the first day?" says Tony. "Remember? You couldn't stop talking. You had to row. 'Tony,' I said to myself, 'this one's gonna be a real pain in the neck.'" Diane gives Larry her hat.

"This is an elemental place," says Larry the philosopher later that evening as we lie in our bags, staring up into the night. "You don't change it. It changes you."

Her Vacation

He ate a hot dog in the Detroit airport and two more when we landed in San Diego. He was playing the role of "condemned man on his way to a spa" to the hilt. In San Diego, a bus picked us up to drive us across the border. The driver told us the bus trip would take about an hour. Good. It was going to be the only hour since we'd left New York that morning that Larry wouldn't have something in his mouth.

The spa had been my idea. It was my turn. It was at his request that we had gone white-water rafting the year before. He could bloody well go to a spa.

Just inside the Mexican border, he spotted a sign:

CARNICERÍA Y ABARROTE — Spanish for butcher and grocery. He got the driver to stop and emerged moments later from the small, dusty supermarket with several bags of Cheetos. He would go to Rancho La Puerta, a vegetarian, aerobic, calorie-counting mountain spa, but he would act like a baby the whole time. Swell! This meant that I would feel like his mother the whole time.

As we drove into the town of Tecate, he peered intently out the window of the bus, sounding out every sign he saw that might indicate the presence of retail food. "Tacos and *pollo!*" he cried out, happy as a child as the bus wound through town. "How far is the spa?"

"About two miles," was the answer.

"Things are looking up," said Larry, hoovering up the first bag of Cheetos. "And look!" he cried, orange dust still clinging to his lips, "a *mueblería!*" The only fun I had that day was telling him that he was salivating over a furniture store.

Vacations have a way of reopening gender issues for us, issues we both thought had been settled years ago. This, after all, is a man who no longer sees anything sexually compromising about so-called women's work. He enjoys washing dishes — "It's the only thing I do all day that has a beginning, a middle, and an end," he likes to say. And he cooks about half the meals we eat. I hate to rub it in, but he even likes to unload the dishwasher. For my part, I cheerfully take out the garbage and drive in England. And yet, after years of fine-tuning our yin and yang, he was suddenly telling me that going to spas was a "girl thing."

"You have to wear tights for yoga," he accused.

"No, you don't," I defended. "You can wear a sweat suit. But you might enjoy wearing tights. They make you feel so stretchy and catlike."

"If I want to feel catlike, I'll get a litter box," he answered, and promptly launched into an indignant monologue on the sociopolitical implications of working out. For one thing, working out was deca-dent. Why didn't people do real work in workout clothes? He had an idea. Spandex tights should be sold to people only if they are willing to do manual labor. Tights would be available in hardware stores, along with hammers, saws, shovels, and trowels. Let the yuppies lift bricks instead of weights. People should work out where they're most needed—in the slums, on bridges and roadways, and in the subways. For all the calories aerobically dissipated into thin air by thousands of Evian-swigging, spandex-wearing narcissists pedaling bikes and climbing stairs to nowhere, we could rebuild the South Bronx! Street crime would be driven into the health clubs.

Nor was he impressed by the fact that William F. Buckley Jr. went to this spa. "That figures," he sneered, implying God knows what, and turned on his heel. "George Hamilton goes!" I yelled after him. "What about that! And Sophia Loren!"

He would not be moved. There was no question about it: he had reverted into manic machismo. I had only to say the word *spa* to trigger a testosterone tantrum. It wasn't just the idea of exercising that made him rant. He also could not bear the thought of eating a no-salt vegetarian diet for a week: "If I want fiber, I'll chew on a rope." For Larry, *spa food* was an oxymoron, like *guest host* or *reasonable attorney's fees*.

Not surprisingly, Larry also had his own theory about dieting. He advocated skipping meals, specifically breakfast and lunch. Dinner, he believed, should be chosen from all seven of the basic food groups—beer, pizza, chocolate, cheese, chicken wings, nachos, and sour cream. It's a diet he adheres to faithfully. It has kept him a consistent ten pounds overweight for years, but then my "anything you eat standing up doesn't count" diet has done the same for me.

As the fatal day approached, Larry seemed to mellow a bit. The ranting stopped. "It's no big deal," he said to me quite calmly. "I'll be fine. While you go to the workout classes, I'll play tennis, I'll swim, I'll take walks, and I'll do a lot of reading."

This blessed state of relative acceptance lasted until we got there. Then group pressure, his natural curiosity, and the bitter knowledge that he had paid for it anyway began to transform him. He attended

his first yoga class. Once there, pure ego sustained him. He could not have failed to notice that he was the strongest, thinnest, best-looking man in the room. Or that he had the most hair. Or that he was the only one who could do the yoga headstand. Nor did it hurt when Michele, the instructor, her buns vivid in neon spandex, asked him if he was a yogi. And I don't think he could have been totally un-moved by the fact that there were a lot of attractive women dragging their mats across the floor to be near him. "You're lucky," one of the nervier ones told me. "Your husband has a wonderful body."

The Spa King's enthusiasm grew stronger the closer he came to being able to touch his toes with-out bending his knees. "Men aren't naturally as flexible as women," he explained to me. "Michele says not to bounce. I should just let the weight of my head gradually pull me down. It helps if you breathe into it."

He was happy. He, who had never studied Spanish, was greeting the Mexican gardeners with a hearty *"Buenos días!"* as he sprinted from Morning Stretch Intermediate to Body Toning Intense. Suddenly he knew from "abs" and "glutes."

I should have been happy, but I wasn't. First of all, I was sore. And second of all, he was too happy. He was going to classes all day and nothing hurt.

"Just breathe into the place," he advised me, the perverse traitor. And third of all, I was the one who was supposed to be good at this. I was the one who had worked out for years. I was the one who could put her head on her knees and put her hand on the bottom of her foot and straighten her leg like a ballet dancer. I was the one with the tights. I was the girl!

And fourth of all, I was hungry.

Fantasy Real Estate

Our passion for travel is fraught with internal contradictions. We travel to go away and to come home. When we travel to foreign lands, we insist upon feeling "at home," never mind that we're surrounded by minarets or rice paddies or alps. And then, to add to the impossibility of our demands, we also refuse to be tourists, in spite of the fact that that's precisely what we are.

It's not enough to be enjoying the culture, eating the food, and drinking the wine; we have to own the place. One minute we're behaving like proper sightseers in Provence, Florence, or Prague, and the next we're house hunting. We travel the way Caesar's

army conquered Gaul: we come, we see, we acquire real estate—at least in our dreams.

When in Rome, Larry the chameleon imagines himself sitting all day outside his apartment in the Piazza Navona. He is sipping cappuccino, reading a book on architecture, and smoking. (Larry resumes smoking on all of his fantasy vacations.) Larry does not have a job in Rome. I don't either, unless diving for coins in the Trevi Fountain counts. In order to keep our fantasy aloft, we have learned to avoid the little pinpricks of reality, such as how we're going to make a living, how fast we can learn the language, what we'll do for friends, whether we can get a referral from our primary care physician, where to redeem our empty soda cans, or what to do with our children.

Not every vacation destination is good fantasy material. It may be a nice place to visit, but even inveterate dreamers wouldn't want to live there. Some places are too hot; some, too cold. I'd be cutting sod in Ireland right now if it weren't for the bloody rain.

We also don't have many Third World real estate fantasies. I hate to think we could be so shallow, but it may be that our ability to have a good fantasy is linked to the life expectancy and gross national product of the country involved. We once went on a "trek" in the Himalayas. I passed scores of women who were also trekking, but they were doing it all day, every day, up and down the mountain, carrying plastic buckets of water on their heads.

The Nepalese fantasy outlook was a little more promising for Larry. The men in the villages spent their days sitting cross-legged, playing cards, smoking, and growing stubble. Sure, I yearned to breathe that pure mountain air on a permanent basis, and to see day break gloriously each morning over Mount Everest—but not with a bucket on my head.

Paris is our all-time favorite place in which to pretend to live. We've almost bought real estate there several times. We don't care if the French aren't friendly. When we are French, we won't be friendly either.

I love to imagine who I'd be if I were French. Would I care to be that flamboyantly hennaed woman carrying the baguette, the one with the cheekbones, the magenta frock, and the green kid heels that do not hurt her feet? I imagine her on her way to the open-air market, where she will buy an armload of flowers and, on a whim, a canary in a cage. (I do not like birds and have never wished to own one, but in Paris I will.)

Larry the lawyer thinks he's that insouciant guy over there, leaning against the archway, rolling a Gauloise around between his lips, letting the ash fall. Larry's Parisian fantasy involves frequent visits to the Louvre, reading in the Tuileries, eating organ meats, and, in the summers, sailing off the coast of Normandy. (Larry doesn't sail and we have lived for thirty years on the coast of Long Island Sound.)

After a few days of imagining ourselves French, we find we are speaking French. That is to say, we are speaking our very own spontaneous patois — using French words when we can remember them, and when we can't, speaking English with a French accent, like Charles Boyer. But of course. We eat a lot of *sandwiches au jambon*. We return to the same café at dusk. We discuss which of our favorite reds should be our house wine.

Thus frenchified, we sense the time is right to find our fantasy a place to live. Invariably, on one of our many delightfully aimless walks, we find ourselves in front of a real estate office. We examine the photos on display in the window. Do we want a house or an apartment? Should we rent or buy, *louer* or *acheter?* The Left Bank, of course, but *quel arrondissement?*

Larry, whose favorite opera is *La Bohème*, would like something in the way of a garret, with a dormer window and chimney pots. And a sink in the corner. I'm not fussy, as long as there's a place for my canary.

But can we afford it?

Larry, the one with a left side to his brain, converts the various asking prices from euros into dollars. These monetary conversions are followed by a pause, which is long and weighty enough to indicate that we are giving sober consideration to the matter. Then he speaks the words that let me know we've got a full-fledged fantasy on our hands: "I wonder how much we could get for our house." We've got liftoff. It is embarrassing to think about the trail of aborted rental and purchase agreements we have left in our vacationing wake. In Saint-Rémy-de-Provence it was "Small house in town with irises and cyprus trees"; in Kathmandu, "Renovated monastery cell"; in Jackson Hole, "Log cabin, Teton backdrop"; in the Cotswolds, "One bedroom cottage, thatched."

How easily we betray our real lives in our dreams!

How heedless of the time and energy we put into home, community, and friends, never mind love of country. Vacation fantasizing is a lot like a midlife crisis: you want to dump your old life and marry some place newer.

We are not the innocent, faithful children we once were. We don't call out a fond "Good-bye, house! Good-bye, door! Good-bye, steps! Good-bye, lawn!" as we back down the driveway. Instead, it's "Lemme outta here," as we make our escape, pursued by a swarm of stress: Did I change the message on the answering machine? Do I have my passport? Did I hold the mail, pay the bills, water the lawn, call off the newspaper, program the VCR, turn down the thermostat, straighten my sock drawer, review my will, forget the tickets, remember the current adapter? Who wouldn't want to live somewhere else?

Most of the time we're pretty good at keeping fantasy in its place. Of course we're not going to live in a garret in Paris. We're just playing house. We've learned our lesson the hard way. Whenever we have tried to mix fantasy with reality, the gods have exacted their price for defying the cosmic order. It can be paid either in cash or in humiliation.

After a particularly pleasant vacation in London a few years ago, we were able to resist the temptation to buy a flat and instead settled for actually buying a London cab. At the time, cabs that had been retired from service were sold at a garage near Elephant and Castle. Ours had over three hundred thousand miles on it. It had a running board. It was full of quaint advertisements. The seat flipped down. The meter worked. We imagined what fun we'd have picking up our friends for dinner and a movie.

Once home, we waited eagerly for the word from Hoboken that our taxi had arrived. When Larry claimed it at the dock, he and three guys with tattoos had to push it to get it started. Then the wheels fell off. The customs inspector felt so sorry for Larry that he refused to charge him any duty.

In 1971, when we were young and idealistic, we trespassed the threshold between fantasy and reality big-time. We moved from Connecticut to Big Sur, California, on the strength of a two-week stay at the Esalen Institute, where I was convinced that I could actualize my human potential by pounding on a pillow and hugging strangers. (This was before E-mail.)

It's not as if our friends didn't try to warn us, but we stubbornly refused to get the point.

"Haven't *you* ever had a fantasy about living a better life in another place?" I asked a friend who was trying his best to stop us.

"Sure I have. I think about moving to London and hiring out as a butler in a well-appointed home," he said. (This was a man whose house was messy and his professional life complicated and unpredictable.)

"Well, then, why don't you do it?" I said.

"Because then I wouldn't have it as a *fantasy* any more."

For an entire year I was a California mountain woman. I went braless. I wore a black leotard and long paisley skirts that could double as tablecloths.

I grew all my hair and made my own granola. I said things like "far out" and "head trip." But no matter what I did or how hard I pounded, I was still from the Northeast.

Larry, who is better than I am at making the best of a bad deal, smoked a lot of Camels and volunteered as a model for the massage class. When we finally got home and slipped back into reality, we vowed we'd never, ever again lose our grip on fantasy. That didn't last long.

Reality Real Estate

We had been dreaming for years about renting a villa in Italy. We imagined a place perched high on a hill, a view of red-tiled rooftops and vineyards below. There would be rosemary growing in the garden, and cozy rooms cluttered with family heirlooms. We'd hang ropes of garlic and a Parma ham in the sunny kitchen and dip crusty bread into a terra-cotta bowl filled with redundantly chaste extra-virgin olive oil. This time we would not be tourists, always on the outside of life, moving from hotel to hotel, packing and unpacking, collecting tiny bottles of shampoo. We'd shop only at farmers' markets: *spaghetti, pomodoro, pecorino, porcini — no problema.* We'd go on picnics. We wouldn't feel the typical tourist compulsion to see everything. We wouldn't stand in line at the Uffizi. We'd stay home, curled up in a cozy armchair, and read all day if we wanted to. We'd stay home and make love all day if we wanted to. And we'd see the Piero della Francescas too.

I pored over a number of rental catalogs, looking at photos and reading descriptions, until I came upon what I was sure would be the rental home of our dreams — "a renovated mill, located in the heart of the Chianti Classico region, only two kilometers from the center of San Gimignano, a hill town famous for its beautiful towers. A perfect base for exploring Tuscany."

In retrospect, the description was accurate as far as it went, although I think the photograph of the living room, featuring the sofa in the foreground, in no way suggested that it was the only piece of furniture in the room. It is true that the catalog never mentioned anything about heirloom furnishings, the view, or rosemary in the garden. Maybe I should have inquired about these specifics. And to be fair, I probably should have known that we would not be looking down on rooftops, or anything else, for that matter, since, as Larry did not hesitate to point out to me rather testily once we got there, "You knew you were renting a converted mill. You know that mills use waterpower. You know that water doesn't flow uphill." Nor was it the agent's fault that it rained every day of our stay, or that I brought the Scrabble set but forgot the tiles, or that Larry started smoking again, or that the fiasco had cost us $1,750.

By the end of our two-week *vacanza* in *purgatorio*, which felt like a year, we thought it only decent to leave a note of warning for the couple from Oregon who had rented the place for the next two weeks.

"*Benvenuto!* We are the Weismans, the people who rented this villa for the two-week period just before yours. We hope you won't look upon this note as an impudent invasion of your privacy, but rather as an act of compassion.

"Welcome to Villa Potemkin. Right about now you must be wondering why the house is so dark;

what happened to the furniture; why there are no rugs on the floors, no spoons in the kitchen, soap in the soap dish, or hangers in the closets; and what to make of the fact that the only art in the house, which hangs over the kitchen table, is a pen-and-ink drawing of a headless man in a sport jacket, holding his own entrails.

"We suggest that you take a look at the 'house book' right away. That's the loose-leaf notebook on the kitchen table, next to the flashlight. It's packed with diagrams, troubleshooting advice, and the phone numbers of people to call in an emergency. The book was written by Villa Potemkin's owner, Nigel Potemkin, who is also a well-known London architect and the man responsible for this millhouse renovation. We learned from Mark, the English caretaker who stops by from time to time to offer his condolences, that Mr. Potemkin is a member of the postmodernist school of English architecture aptly known as the New Brutalism. Prince Charles, who is very concerned with preserving Britain's architectural legacy, has spoken out often against the

deconstructionist vogue, but his words have failed to deter Mr. Potemkin.

"Nicoletta is the name of the housekeeper. She comes in every Saturday to hose down the floors, strip the beds, and change the batteries in the flashlights. Nicoletta has mixed feelings about the New Brutalism. 'This is easy place to clean,' she says, 'but hard place to live in.'

"As you are bound to discover, the house book, although detailed and informative, is irrelevant or incomplete in too many instances. Don't bother to read the chapter titled 'How to Operate the Cappuccino Machine.' The machine does not *va bene* any longer, having blown up several rentals ago.

"Familiarize yourself especially with the text and diagrams on page 15, under 'Electrical Problems': 'If electrical supply cuts out, set restart button on incoming supply. If electrical supply cuts out to ground floor only, set internal restart button.' This information will prove particularly important if you're renting the villa during the rainy season, which you are. We know that the guidebooks say that September and October are ideal months to visit Tuscany and that the Italian rainy season begins in early November and lasts through December, but Nicoletta disagrees. She says that for the last few years the rainy season has occurred early, in September and October.

"The Italian rainy season is very impressive, very operatic. *Che tempo orribile!* (What awful weather!) Very vivace, very fortissimo, very agitato, with molte, molte blown fuses *(lampadina bruciata)*. The instructions in the house book are fine as far as they go, but they won't help you once you have an Italian-speaking electrician on the other end of the phone.

"An ordinary tourist can get by on *'Grazie'* ('Thank you'), 'Per favore' ('Please'), and *'Dov'è il gabinetto?'* ('Where is the bathroom?'). You, however, will need to know how to say, *'Dov'è la valvola?'* ('Where is the restart button?').

"All Italian appliances have *valvolas*. At any time, any one of them may be hit by lightning. Don't be surprised if you find yourself asking *'Dov'è la valvola? Dov'è la valvola?'* with metronomic regularity. Try it to the tune of 'La donna è mobile.'

"In addition to the information above, which we trust will be useful, Larry and I have attempted to anticipate some of the questions that may arise during your stay.

"*Where is the view?* Not everyone who rents a villa in a hill town in Tuscany automatically gets a view. *Somebody's* got to live in the valleys. Villa Potemkin is located at the bottom of a valley, at the end of a two-kilometer rutted dirt driveway, so steep, winding, and narrow that it must be executed in first gear, and then only under dry, daytime conditions. You will get used to life in a hole. So you don't have a view of acres of rolling vineyards, rows of stately cypress trees, and the charmingly scabby ocher farmhouses with their red tile roofs. You're a part of somebody else's view. You're somebody else's red tile roof!

"Why is the underside of my rental car making that funny noise? Parts of it are falling off. See 'Where is the view?' above.

"Are there screens for the windows, to keep out flies and those long, gray things that have wings and jump? No.

"Where is the nearest garden market? There is no nearest garden market. There's an A & P about twelve kilometers from San Gimignano (not counting the driveway). A & P went to Italy at about the same time D'Agostino's came to New York. It costs five hundred lire to rent a shopping cart. That's the silver coin with the copper center. *Risotto ai funghi porcini* comes in a plastic bag with directions to

drop the contents into *'acqua in ebollizione.'* It's *'pronto in l5 minuti.'* (So many of the words are the same.) The Parmesan is grated. The tomatoes come from New Jersey. The bakery sells croissants. Take a number.

"Why does the shower fill up and pour under the bathroom door and run down the hallways? Because there is hair in the drain.

"Why does our hair feel so thin and lifeless? Because the house has its own well and there are *chimici nell'acqua* (chemicals in the water). That's *your* hair in the drain.

"Why is there an echo? What else would you expect from a virtually unfurnished, renovated mill with barrel-vaulted ceilings as high as major duomos, thirty-two stone steps, a living room the size of the Roman Forum, a fireplace in which you could roast a wild boar—if it weren't bricked over—and no drapes. A cast-iron sofa, a slate kitchen table, two folding chairs, two metal beds, and a broken cappuccino machine don't provide much acoustic relief under those conditions. We both should have asked

---

the agent to send us pictures of the *inside* of the house. We actually considered buying a sofa and a couple of chairs in nearby Siena. Furniture, the more upholstered the better, would absorb sound and act as a wind barrier as well. Some rugs on the terra-cotta tile floors and a few tapestries on the gray plaster walls would also help to cut down on the echo. Or you can just stop talking to each other. That's what we did. Plus we drank a lot of Chianti Classico."

The Summer Houseguest

Not all our rental experiences are disasters. For several summers we leased a cunning gray-shingled summer cottage directly on the beach on Cape Cod. Renting somebody else's life is the most convenient way to have our fantasy and leave it too. Living in other people's homes, cooking in other people's kitchens, even doing other people's dishes, has the allure of novelty that is at the heart of any leased vacation experience.

We intentionally chose a place that was a total contrast to the way we live at home. The furniture was authentic battered wicker. The once-flowered cushions were bleached to a pastel wash by years of insistent sunlight. Chaste white muslin curtains flapped at the windows. In the kitchen, cups and dishes of various sizes and patterns, some fetchingly chipped, were arranged in cozy stacks on open wooden shelves. The paint on the pine-plank kitchen table had been worn away by years of scrubbing, leaving only faint traces of Wedgwood blue clinging to the grain. On top of the table sat a sparkling glass pitcher of chilled lemonade, beads of condensation clinging to its curved surface. The place was three thousand dollars for the month of August. Ralph Lauren would have paid a lot more for a one-day photo shoot.

We would leave behind our workaday lives of rushing, getting, spending, and narcoleptic television viewing. Clothing wouldn't matter. We would spend the day in our bathing suits. Nor would food. We'd buy our dinner from the local fishermen. Instead of swimming a mile's worth of laps at the Westport Y, we'd swim in the bay, to the lighthouse and back. We'd read on the deck, walk on the beach, pick up shells, and watch the stars. The idea was to reduce life to its basic elements and simple joys.

We didn't count on the houseguests. It is not possible to rent a beach house within five hours' drive of one's hometown without being visited by people. This is especially true if I have actually invited them.

One of my problems is that I like to be nicer than I actually am. While this personality discrepancy is

better than being unkind, it does create a lot of confusion and pain for me as well as for others. I mean well, at least initially. I miss my friends. I want to see you. I want to show you this darling cottage and share all the fun we're having. Then, after about an hour, I want you to go home.

After the Labor Day weekend, when the last of the summer houseguests has thanked us for a lovely weekend, gotten into the car, and driven away, leaving us with an empty refrigerator, dirty sheets, soggy towels, and something we will have to find a box for and mail back to them, I am moved to boot up my laptop and bang out a hostess note that, if I had the nerve to mail it, would solve my summer houseguest problem forever.

"Dear Summer Houseguests,

"Now that the summer season has passed, here in our rented beach house, Larry and I want to take this opportunity to thank you for being such perfect guests, and to reiterate the house rules so that your visit next summer, should we rent again, may prove to be an even greater success.

"*What to bring.* You will need a bathing suit, a toothbrush, dental floss in case of native corn, your own sunblock, and proof of passage back to where you came from. Travel lightly. Steamer trunks will be confiscated. I am not Jane Austen. Yours is not to be a visit of nineteenth-century duration.

"*The house gift.* It is necessary to bring a small offering, preferably a large, cooked meal that can be eaten cold with the fingers, along with a good supply of paper plates. An SUV-ful of zucchini from your garden is not welcome and will be considered a hostile, provocative act. A new blender is an especially thoughtful idea. Last summer's blender, you will remember, burned itself out in a valiant five-speed attempt at pesto sauce. This is probably as good a time as any to let you know that we lied about the chewy little white chunks that clung to the linguini. They were not unosterized pignoli. A white rubber spatula also makes a nice house gift.

"*Meals.* There will be a traditional welcoming dinner of corn on the cob and lobster. Further meals will not be provided. Do not be fooled by the splendor of this meal or the graciousness of your hosts. You are on hospitality death row. Make the most of it. Let me butter your corn. Larry will insist upon cracking your claws.

"*Help.* Do not offer to help us clear the table. Don't even pretend to get up from your place; we'll slam you back down in your chair. By Saturday breakfast, even before the zinnias we put on your night table begin to wilt, you're on your culinary own. The coffee's in the refrigerator, and the filter papers are on the pantry shelf. I take mine black with half a teaspoon of sugar. Larry likes a little milk.

"*Make yourself at home.* Whenever you get hungry, you should feel free to help yourselves to whatever is in the pantry or the refrigerator. Now it is our turn to pretend to hoist ourselves up from our lounge chairs and yours to insist that you will not be waited upon. Make your choice quickly. Do not open the door and stare. Whenever the refrigerator door is opened, a light goes on in me. Although as a hostess I am by now certifiably brain-dead, the twenty-five-watt glow reflected off the white interior enamel produces the same effect upon me, splayed out on my chaise, as an electrode applied to the nerves of a formaldehyde frog on a laboratory table. I twitch with phantom hostess guilt. (Larry doesn't do guilt; he just won't get up.) If you do not conclude within seconds that there is nothing to eat except baking soda, I will feel compelled to assist you to that conclusion by reciting the contents of the refrigerator and the pantry: 'Mayo, but no tuna; salsa, but no chips; a humid box of Grape-Nuts—and if I were you, I'd smell the milk.'

"When you're at home and you have no food, you go shopping. When you're making yourself at home in our home and there's no food, you should also go shopping. The A & P, which is air-conditioned, is a mile and one-half down the road on the right and is a nice place to visit, especially at low tide. Remember, I don't eat bluefish, Larry doesn't eat anything that flies, and you use a lot of paper towels. While you're there, would you please pick up two copies of the newspaper so that Larry won't have to erase your crossword puzzle?

"*Laundry.* There is no laundry. There are no towels. In the event that wetness occurs after swimming or showering, guests are requested to jump up and down on the deck until the condition clears up. In order that subsequent guests may also enjoy clean sheets, please sleep on top of the bedspread.

"*Conversation.* We will not ask you if you had a good night's sleep if you will not ask us. Keep all remarks before 9:00 A.M. to a simple 'Good morning.' Since we are not responsible for the weather but only feel as if we are, statements like 'I love a rainy day at the beach' are regarded as insincere and passive-aggressive. So are the questions 'Is there anything I can do?' and 'Where do you keep the ice cubes?' Unwelcome topics of conversation include periodic reports that you are 'unwinding.' (You are not unwinding; you are feeling the first heady symptoms of malnutrition.) Larry particularly resents estimates of the height of the stack of mail that awaits you on your desk. Please be especially careful not to tell us how lucky we are to be able to be on vacation for a whole month. We are not on vacation. We are entertaining you. Permissible subjects of conversation include our dreams, my tan, and your stretch marks.

"*Weather.* After two consecutive days of rain, the impulse to go home is a healthy one and should be acted upon.

"*Your departure.* Do not strip the bed. (See 'Laundry,' above.) Do not leave anything behind. If you do, you may buy it back next Wednesday between 11:00 A.M. and 4:00 P.M. from the Sisters of the Immaculate Visitation at Saint Mary's by the Harbor thrift shop.

"*Off-season communications.* If either of us should, in the course of speaking with you during the winter months, even suggest the possibility that we might rent a cottage again next summer, please be good enough not to remind us of it next spring."

Having a Terrible Time

We like to think that we choose our vacation destinations freely, but in fact, most of the time the choice is made for us by the elusive, fickle finger of fashion. Countries, like children's names, go in and out of fashion: *Tiffany* gives way to *Nicole; Matthew* to *Jason*. Suddenly it's time to talk Turkey, rent a villa in Tuscany or an apartment in London, cruise to Alaska, or visit Belize, a country we hadn't even heard of. At the turn of this new century, travelers, lemminglike, were converging en masse on Antarctica. We haven't yet visited Antarctica, or the North Pole, Australia, New Zealand, or China. Larry, of course, is raring to go, but I resist.

As I get older, these places seem to be moving farther away. They have come to constitute their own special category on my list of future trips: too far to go, but not too far to have been.

If there's any criterion by which one might predict America's next popular vacation spot, it may be our enthusiasm for visiting countries with which we've recently been at war or which have otherwise been brought to their knees—Russia, Vietnam, Cambodia, and, any minute now, Afghanistan. If Hilton builds in Tora Bora, will they come?

When we decided to go to Chile a few years ago, we found ourselves ahead of the fashion curve. We didn't know it at the time, but we were the trendsetters, the Joneses up with whom others would soon have to keep. We were surprised that the consistent response to our choice of that particular destination was, "What made you go *there?*"

Nobody ever asks, "Why France?" "Why Italy?" or "Why England?" Visiting England is like visiting your mom. She's old and has nice manners, cheap theater tickets, and lots of curious old relics in her attic that are fun to look at over and over again, like Westminster Abbey, the Tower of London, and Buckingham Palace. Best of all, she speaks English, she loves us, and she's finally learned how to cook. Chile, apparently, is a different story.

Everybody knows why Ferdinand Magellan went to Chile. For him, it was a natural: he was looking for the Strait of Magellan. Nazi-hunters were looking for Martin Bormann. Drug runners go to Chile looking for dope. But why did we go? I blame it on the laundry and my lifelong tendency to get carried away.

I am a romantic. I'm a pushover for a good-looking landscape—a craggy peak, an arid desert, or a frozen tundra. Just whisper "Tierra del Fuego" in my ear and I am instantly aroused and unable to resist the call of the wild or pay attention to the voice of reason saying, "You hate cold, you hate windy, you hate uninhabited."

It is my practice to unload the contents of the dryer onto our king-size bed and fold the darks and lights neatly into piles of his and hers, all the while distracting myself from the tedium of the chore by watching television.

This particular afternoon, I viewed a travel documentary on Chile. There, before my marveling eyes, I saw people who could have been me or Larry sand-boarding down the sand dunes in the Atacama Desert in northern Chile. It looked like such fun!

By the time I had matched all the socks, I was transported to the center of Chile, where the same happy people were poised at the edge of the volcano-rimmed waters of Chile's stunning Lake District. Just one commercial later, they were in Patagonia, and it was there that I became one with them, galloping through the rugged wilderness. In the background were the mountain peaks I would climb the next morning, after I got off my horse.

This was the most extraordinarily gorgeous country I'd ever seen! I had to go! So intense was my desire that it honestly didn't cross my mind until we got to Chile six months later that I was now sixty-three years old and I had never ridden a horse. Nor, for that matter, had I ever gone surfboarding on water, never mind sand, or climbed a mountain. And, by the way, Larry, who knew how to do all three, hadn't bothered to remind me of this, which is another reason that he had a very good time in Chile and I did not.

Larry doesn't care where he goes on vacation; for him, *go* and *vacation* are the operative words. Larry will travel anywhere to do anything, and no matter

what happens, he'll have a wonderful time. I tend to think this is because he is basically much less sensitive and discriminating than I am, although, to be fair, he might say it's because he is essentially a much happier, more open-minded, and less demanding and judgmental person.

Given our division of labor—he does nothing, I do everything—I was the one who spent hours on the phone with my on-line travel agent, insisting that there was too such a thing as sand-boarding in the Atacama Desert, that I had seen it on a TV documentary, that it was practically my main reason for spending a small fortune to go to Chile, and that I would cancel the trip if she couldn't locate someone

to rent us sand boards, whatever they were, and find us a suitable dune.

However, when we actually got there, it was Larry who was able, in spite of the high altitude, to drag himself and his sand board up a two-hundred-foot sand dune, strap his feet sideways, one in front of the other, onto a narrow strip of wood, keep his balance while keeping his knees bent, and slide smartly down the sandy incline. I was the one who stood at the bottom taking pictures of his many descents. (It wasn't as if I didn't try to sand-board. Stopping to take a rest and a swig from my water bottle at six-inch intervals, I made it halfway up the dune. I even strapped my feet onto the board at an angle and succeeding in assuming an upright position before I realized that I had already had arthroscopic surgery in one knee and it would make a lot more sense if I just sat down and pretended I was on a toboggan. This proved humiliatingly ineffective since sand is not like snow, my behind is several inches wider than the board, and even after giddy-apping my heels vigorously and repeatedly into the dune, nothing budged.)

Larry and I love to swim. It seemed only natural that I make careful arrangements with our travel agent to make sure we had an opportunity to go swimming during our two-day visit to the Lake District in central Chile.

It had not escaped my notice that the lakes might be fed by runoff from the surrounding snow-covered volcanoes and therefore might be prohibitively cold. After all, no one was swimming in the documentary. "What," I asked my beleaguered agent, "is the average temperature of the water in February?" After making a number of contacts with her people in Chile, the word came back: somewhere between fifty-five and sixty-two degrees.

"Is that Fahrenheit?" I pressed, just to be sure. (Large issues, such as "Do I really want to go to Chile, or is viewing the documentary enough?" tend to escape my notice, but when it comes to the details, I'm a terrier.)

We would need wet suits. The research for the perfect suits began in the yellow pages and quickly moved on-line, where I located two at $375 apiece and had them mailed on approval. Assisted by each other and a spray can of PAM, Larry and I were able to struggle into ours in under a half hour, which is OK if you're not competing in a triathlon. The wet suits took up so much space in our luggage that we had to ditch our foul-weather gear, which, it turned out, we could have used in the third and last part of the trip, while mountain climbing in the freezing-cold, wind-driven rainstorms in Patagonia.

Unfortunately, by the time we got to the Lake District, I was already suffering from insomnia, which can be brought on by changing time zones, being at high altitudes, and having a bad time. I was spending my days yawning and watching Larry have fun, and my nights sitting up in bed, watching him sleep. It is not easy maintaining good sportsmanship, never mind a marriage, under these conditions.

Meanwhile Larry, who insists upon preserving all of his bodily functions no matter where he is or how hostile or disruptive the circumstances might be, especially for others whom he is supposed to care about, remained oblivious to my condition.

"Did you have a good night's sleep?" he'd ask each morning.

"I was up all night," I'd say—not to make him feel bad or guilty, but just because it was true. After all, if you're not going to be honest with the person you love, especially when you're on vacation together, well, then, what's the point?

"Funny, you were snoring at five A.M. when I got up to pee," he'd say, planting a little kiss on my cheek, throwing back the covers, and leaping out of bed.

What would this vacation have been like, I wondered, if I were on my own? I might have met someone who enjoyed planning vacations, so that I could have just relaxed and had a good time. I might have met a guy who didn't spy on me at night and didn't know how to sand-board, someone with whom I might have had something in common, like insomnia.

I was too tired to swim that day; I stayed in the hotel, which I had specifically selected because it was located on the best lake, and watched Larry. The water temperature was sixty-five. He didn't wear his wet suit. He swam two miles. I didn't take any pictures.

Our next and final stop was Patagonia. Although Patagonia is located in *el sud*, it is nevertheless the coldest part of Chile. It is almost in Antarctica. This counterintuitive situation is caused by the equator, which has a way of disorienting people who live above it into thinking that *south* means hot and *north* means cold.

Nor had I fully absorbed the idea that when you are ineluctably drawn to words like *remote outpost,* you have to figure that there are no commercial landing fields nearby. The item on our itinerary that read "Fly to Punta Arenas, transfer by van (six hours) to your hotel" had escaped my notice. Romantics tend to skip over parenthetical information.

Although I had made all the arrangements to stay in a hotel that had a stable, it was Larry who went galloping off into the Patagonian pampas on his silver steed, leaving me slumped on the beginner's nag, led around on a string by a grouchy gaucho who apparently wasn't being paid enough to kick my horse in the flanks from time to time, just to keep him walking.

I had reached my limit. Larry was having fun on purpose. He obviously didn't give a damn what happened to me. Larry, who would be spending his vacation at home doing crossword puzzles if it weren't for me, had abandoned me. After all I'd done, he could have stayed by my side and kept me company.

Or at the very least he could have had the decency to remind me that I don't know how to ride a horse.

Telling

Nobody wants to hear about your vacation unless you've had a terrible time. Then they're all ears. Even people who like you can stand just so much of your gaseous descriptions of swimming in the warm Gulf of Mexico waters or strolling on the Île Saint-Louis. After a few minutes their eyes glaze over and their smiles become fixed, indicating that you've used up their allotted quotient of niceness.

Other people's numbing recitatives are about as entertaining as listening to descriptions of a meal one didn't eat, a dream one didn't have, a book one didn't read, or a marriage in which nobody cheated or argued, saw a therapist, or had anything other than missionary sex.

While I kind of like the annual Christmas photos some of our friends send us, assembled with their kids and dog in front of the hearth, I have yet to get through the accompanying two-page, single-spaced letter about how interesting their lives are, how achieving their children, and how golden their retriever.

There is in fact a "Don't ask, don't tell" rule of travel. The only exception to it is self-interest: if your friends happen to be going where you've just been, then they are desperate to know if you had a wonderful time—did you go on your own or did you take a tour, is it better to go for two weeks or is ten days enough, how was the food, and may they borrow your maps and travel guides, which they will not return.

Larry thinks this fondness for other people's bad trips reflects poorly on early childhood education in America, particularly the time wasted on show-and-tell, but I don't agree. I think what we're dealing with here is nothing less than *Schadenfreude* — the dark side of human nature, the same post-Edenic state that compels us to pass up the local newspaper with the headline COUPLE CELEBRATES 60 YEARS OF WEDDED BLISS in favor of the tabloid news, BOY TRAPPED IN REFRIGERATOR EATS OWN FOOT. Actually, didn't Tolstoy say it best in the opening lines of *Anna Karenina* when he nearly wrote, "Happy vacations are all alike; every unhappy vacation is unhappy in its own way"? This is why we never talk about our vacations unless we have something awful to say.

Larry and I are good at anecdotes, which is not surprising, since we're both shamelessly outgoing, like a lot of attention, and are inclined to exaggerate — traits that give us a natural advantage when it comes to holding an audience. Besides, we use a lot of gestures.

There's more to a good anecdote than a bad time. If you insist upon telling about your trip, you owe it to your reluctant audience to tell it well. Basically it's an acting job. You've got to throw yourself into it. If you're not willing to get out there in the middle of somebody's living room and actually show how you tripped over the gondolier's oar, fell into the canal, and came up with a bit of prosciutto caught behindyour ear, then forget it.

Very often we take a tag-team approach. I tell stories about Larry that he would be too embarrassed or humble to reveal, and he does the same for me. For instance, Larry does me honking and flapping around a restaurant in Japan in an attempt to order duck because the menu was in Japanese and no one spoke English. He has recently added my attempt at sand-boarding to his repertoire.

One of our best-loved anecdotes involves a visit to an Egyptian gynecologist the summer of our protracted honeymoon. (On that trip alone we stockpiled enough hair-raising experiences to capture the conversational flag at a lifetime of social gatherings.)

We were in Greece and I was suffering from what I thought was morning sickness, attributable to that careless night in a tent on the Lido. (We don't reenact that part of the story.)

Because the Greek phone book is in Greek, Larry

had the good idea of calling the American Embassy to see if he could locate a gynecologist. This was going to be a cinch, we figured. After all, *gynecologist* was a Greek word; Athens must be full of them. In fact, the name we got from the marine on duty was that of an Egyptian doctor.

I do the description of the doctor's waiting room. It is a seraglio. It is painted red. There are ferns everywhere. (I do "ferns everywhere" with gestures.) Then I do the doctor pushing aside the purple beaded curtain with great élan, bowing at the waist, and inviting me into his office. (Larry says my charade is more Boris Karloff than Egyptian gynecologist, but our friends seem to like it.) I also do Larry hastening after me, and the part where the doctor asks if it is customary in our country for the husband to accompany his wife into the examining room.

Then Larry takes over for the mortifying part. He does the doctor unhitching my bra, helping me step out of my underpants, and escorting me to an examination table on which I am to recline, as nude and undraped as Manet's Olympia.

Larry skips telling about the actual examination, which was reassuringly professional, and concludes the story with the doctor ripping off his rubber gloves and announcing to an entirely clothed Larry and a totally nude me that I am pregnant. For the finale, Larry demonstrates how they both help me back into my clothes.

When telling travel anecdotes, we think it's best to adhere to the Aristotelian rule of the three unities, which have given Greek tragedy its timeless appeal. All such dramas must offer the following: action (a single theme without episodes or nonessential subplots); place (no changes in setting, which would destroy the illusion); and time (all action to take place within a single twenty-four-hour period). We are also guided by his theories about the importance of *hamartia* (error); *hubris* (pride), our most persistent tragic flaw; and *katharsis* (emotional cleansing), the element that gives the satisfactory ending necessary to every tragedy. We find these dramatic principles hold up as well today as they did twenty-three hundred years ago in Thebes.

Our Moroccan adventure was a paradigm of the three unities. We set out from Marrakech in the spring of 1969. Our destination was Ouarzazate (pronounced something like "where's it at") an oasis town in the Sahara. The trip involved taking a road over the High Atlas Mountains, which, according to our map, was a distance of two inches or 124 kilometers. Allowing for the fact that the line on the map was extremely wiggly, we figured it would take us two to three hours (*hamartia*—a major error).

We paid no attention to the description of the drive in *Fodor's* (big-time *hubris*): "The road clings for dear life to the side of the mountain. The mountain trails are not well maintained and numerous streams flow across them. Drive carefully and make sure your vehicle has enough clearance underneath." If we'd gone on a tour, we would have known that the trip was longer than we'd expected, and we would have brought food and water, since there were no restaurants, never mind roadside stands, along the way where we might purchase food—not even a Berber King.

But we don't go on tours. The idea of going on vacation with strangers to see fascinating sights selected for us by people who know the territory, and to be escorted from place to place by experts who speak the language and whose job it is to look out for our comfort, well-being, and happiness, has always struck me as very limiting.
Can three meals a day, a hotel room each night, and an itinerary of well-planned events in between allow enough opportunity for the missed connections, bad meals, holiday closings, and alfresco sleeping

that give a vacation texture? The tour is the enemy of the anecdote.

The people we passed as we clung for dear life to the side of the mountain might as well have been living in the Neolithic period. (This is, of course, an exaggeration. While their houses were made of mud bricks, most of the people were wearing plastic flip-flops. Nor do we mention the telephone lines that ran along the roadway.)

After several hours we were hungry and thirsty. We spotted some robed men on their lunch break, squatting by the side of the road, eating from a pot cooking over an open fire. Luckily their second language was the same as ours—rudimentary French. We asked if there was any place nearby to buy some food. They invited us to share theirs.

I had seen recipes for shepherd's pie in cookbooks, but this was the real thing except that the sheep were goats and the shepherds were goatherds. There was the flock. Here was the stew. Here also was the spoon we shared. We dipped into the communal pot and ate our fill (*hamartia* number two). At this point in the narrative we hunker down and do a little pantomime of spoon sharing and stew eating.

If we had been on a tour, the guide would have warned us that by eating goat stew, no matter how good it looked and tasted, we were risking intestinal distress and possibly a lifelong appetite for tin cans. Until this point, either Larry or I have delivered the narrative, a role that in Aristotle's time would have been handled by the Greek chorus. Now we become the dramatis personae and engage in a little dialogue.

"Is it true," says Larry, taking the part of a goatherd, "that the United States has landed a man on the Moon?"

"*Bien sûr*," I answer.

"They refused to believe us," says Larry, doing a good imitation of our hosts, alternately pointing to the sky, laughing out loud, and then slapping their thighs, making it clear that they knew we were only fooling. They might be Neolithic, but they weren't born yesterday.

Our friends who have been on guided tours to Morocco like to tell about the Mamounia Hotel, the

Casbah, the spice market, and what a deal they got on a living room rug, but they don't stand a chance next to our narrative of our first night in Ouarzazate, competing for the only toilet in the hotel.

We are Lucille Ball and Desi Arnaz as we act out *this*, the climax of the story. We race down a pretend hall, our faces contorted into masks of anguish. Larry pushes me out of the way. I push him out of the way. I try to trip him; he tries to trip me. He pretend slams and locks the bathroom door. I pretend bang and kick it. Talk about emotional cleansing! It's a *katharsis* Aristotle himself would have envied.

A Walk on the Wild Side

When we approached our sixties, we began to understand why the root meaning of the word *travel* is "travail." China, a country we had meant to visit years ago, seemed to be slipping farther and farther out of range, becoming harder and harder to get to. So were Australia and New Zealand, two more on our well-intentioned list of future destinations. Friends our age were beginning to modify their travel plans and go on age-appropriate trips. Cruises were becoming a popular option.

"They have everything on board you could possibly want," reported a couple who came back from what had been advertised as "the ultimate seven-day cruise." The ship boasted a nine-hole miniature golf course, a theater, conference rooms, a library, eight different restaurants, including an all-night diner, a jogging track, three swimming pools, a mall, and a fully equipped gym with twenty treadmills—all with an ocean view. It was so ultimate a cruising experience, they said, that you would swear you were on dry land. It was Westport, Connecticut, floating. We couldn't see the point.

Other friends whose taste in travel was more like our own were signing on for Elderhostel programs and loving them. "They plan everything for you," they said. "They make all the reservations, and you don't have to drive or carry your luggage."

We weren't ready for the vacation equivalent of assisted living, but we couldn't help noticing that we were losing some of our youthful get-up-and-go. Ogden Nash was right: "Middle age is when you're sitting at home on Saturday night and the telephone rings and you hope it isn't for you." We issued audible sighs of relief when we returned to our house at the end of each day. Our favorite destination was turning out to be in bed with a book, our legs intertwined. More and more we were tempted to stay in our own time zone, live in our own home, sleep in our own bed, and not trip over unfamiliar furniture and crack into walls when we needed to visit the bathroom in the middle of the night.

Nevertheless we were determined not to yield to entropy. Before it was too late, we would take our vacations in physically challenging environments and save the easy-to-get-to urban destinations for when we were really old. Afternoon concerts in Saint Martin-in-the-Fields could wait.

To celebrate my sixtieth birthday, we decided we would vacation in the Costa Rican rain forest. Until then, our experience with the jungle had been limited to monkeys at the zoo and toucans on the Froot Loops box. The real jungle, we suspected, wasn't so tame. We decided against the trip that promised the opportunity to boil our own drinking water and sleep overnight in an open tree house. The boiling water part might have been tolerable.

What queered it for me was the prospect of sleeping in an open tree house. Open to what? Monkeys? Snakes? Larry didn't even bother to argue the point. Instead we chose to stay at a resort, described as "the most deluxe jungle and beach hideaway in Costa Rica." The oxymoronic pairing of the adjective *luxury* with the noun *jungle* appealed to our bipolar travel style.

The resort was more than just a pretty place. It was a "model of sustainable ecotourism," a demonstration of how to save the rain forest by enticing nature lovers to pay to see it. Could we qualify as ecotourists? We can't identify anything beyond the generic—tree, rock, bird, bug, vine. We have never counted birds. We are, however, very good about recycling newspapers and anything plastic with a *1* or a *2* on the bottom.

Upon our arrival we were instructed in the ways of living in harmony with the jungle. One rule made a particular impression on me: Don't kill or scream at anything. This meant that if I were soaping up in the outdoor shower and I looked up and saw a monkey hanging from the shower rod, grinning at me, I should smile back. Or if I were to find a beetle the size of a hamburger with many, many legs in my room, I should scoop it up gently and place it out-doors. Actually, I did find such a beetle making his way strenuously across the bedroom floor, and I did ask Larry to "take it out." Unfortunately he watches a lot of Clint Eastwood movies and almost "took it

out" by squashing it under his sneaker. I reminded him just in time that we were ecotourists.

A guided tour of the jungle has much to teach the neoecotourist. First of all, it really is a jungle out there. People actually do hack their way through the underbrush with machetes, sleep under mosquito netting, and get bitten by scorpions. The jungle truly is unimaginably hot and humid. Remember how Sidney Greenstreet and Ava Gardner used to sweat in spite of the overhead fans? Even Tarzan had problems acclimating to jungle life. Had I given the matter sufficient thought, I might have realized that eight degrees from the equator in the middle of a Costa Rican rain forest might not be the optimum vacation destination for a redheaded Caucasian, especially one whose ancestors actually did come from the Caucasus, just outside of Kiev. I might also have figured out that every day is a bad hair day in Costa Rica unless you're Costa Rican.

I learned many lessons from the jungle. For instance, it is very unlikely that Tarzan could have swung from vines, since most are only looped over branches. Also, it is difficult to tell a root from a snake until you've tripped over it, and howler monkeys sound like hound dogs. A butterfly seldom lives longer than three months, and unless you want to further shorten its life, don't pick it up by its wings. Better you should grab it out of thin air by the thorax. And lastly, it is very muddy underfoot and quite humiliating to slide on your butt past the other ecotourists on the trail—hearty honeymooners Robin and Hal from Denver, a holistic optometrist from Park Slope, and Larry.

Another important lesson I learned from the jungle is that it's very nice to be at the top of the food chain. For instance, I am glad that I am not a leaf cutter ant, the insect that gets my vote for the lower species most in need of an intellectual, evolutionary upgrade. Stop to mop your brow at almost any step along the jungle trail, look down, and you will notice what appears to be an endless, slow-moving line of small ants, each bearing a hunk of leaf many times the size of its body. We followed one such line of tiny trudgers for at least a kilometer through the jungle to their destination—a hole in the ground. We observed each of the bearer ants disappearing into the same hole in the ground to deposit its bit of leaf and then heading back in the opposite direction to get another. While my ecotourist companions marveled at the sheer determination of these tiny creatures, I indulged in ecologically incorrect fantasies, such as imagining what would happen if I pushed a stick into the hole. I also wondered as I stood there watching this labor of lug, why, after all these eons, the ants hadn't realized that if they reorganized as a bucket brigade they could deliver more leaf bits faster, thereby freeing up some leisure time in which they could go to the gym, rent a video, or contemplate the meaning of life.

After three hours in the jungle, I had seen, in addition to lots of ants, two black widow spiders, one set of jaguar prints, a gang of spider monkeys swinging high above, and the bottom half of a three-toed mother sloth hanging in a tree—all through binoculars. Another thing ecotourists should know is that any species you see in the jungle you can see much closer up on TV. Of course, you won't be seeing them in their natural habitat. On the other hand, you will be in yours.

My natural habitat turned out to be my bungalow, where I would lie in bed reading, sipping a mango daiquiri, cooled by a ceiling fan, under a canopy of mosquito netting. When I wasn't in bed, I was cooling off in the pool or eating well in the dining room. After day one, I opted out of the eco part of ecotourism. Me no Jane.

Larry of the Jungle—formerly Sir Lawrence of Suburbia—was too alpha-male to give up so quickly. He plunged back into the jungle the next day for the medicine walk, led by the local shaman. Larry staggered out three hours later, and after emptying his boots, showering, and taking three ibuprofen, he crawled in alongside me, under the mosquito netting.

"The shaman called me 'old white man,'" he said before slipping into an exhausted sleep.

Saint Martin-in-the-Fields was beginning to look good.

Coming of Age in Elderhostel

ou folks must be here for the Elderhostel program," said the gentleman behind the reception desk. He said this without the slightest hint of doubt, as if we looked our age, as if we belonged here with these old people, milling about the Atheneum Hotel at the Chautauqua Institution in upstate New York. Was there something wrong with his eyesight?

Elderhostel programs, read the catalog, are for people aged fifty-five and up. Up to what, they do not say. Larry and I are sixty-four and sixty-five respectively, so I suppose it might be said that we qualify.

As much as I do not like getting older, I especially do not like being seen as a member of a designated age group, especially the final one. I do not want to be part of a cohort whose members are called senior citizens, as if they were overdecorated officers in a production of *The Pirates of Penzance.* Nor can I be anything but suspicious of an age group that has to offer its potential members discounts in order to get them to join. Am I being bribed, rewarded, or banished?

Larry, at least regarding the issue of aging, is the saner of us. He takes the discount and runs, for one thing. For another, he has fully absorbed the fact that he is getting old—I think he figured it out the first time he almost didn't recognize his reflection in a shop window. Me? I like to think AARP is the sound a dog makes.

Larry also thinks that since aging is inevitable, it is therefore in one's own best interests to accept it, even to embrace it, instead of clinging pathetically to the notion that one is always and forever the youngest person in the room. He's been sneaking

into the movies as a senior citizen for years. "Two seniors," he says, and they let us both in.

The man in reception handed us each a key to the room, a name card on a chain saying who we were and where we came from, and a schedule of events. He asked us to turn in our car keys. Parking, he told us, was not allowed on the narrow streets of Chautauqua. Our car would be taken to an outlying lot. We could send for it whenever we wished.

So many people had signed up for the five-day lecture program, "American Diplomacy in the Twenty-first Century," that we'd been divided into four groups, each with forty members. The groups were named after pastel colors. We were in the blue group.

One glance at the schedule told me that older people like to run themselves ragged on vacation. Breakfast was at 7:00 A.M. The bus left the hotel at 8:45 for the first lecture, which was at 9:00 A.M. That wasn't going to give me enough time to eat breakfast, wait for the Celebrex to take effect, tie my Dyna-Bands onto the bedpost, do my rotator cuff exercises, and walk to the first lecture. (I wouldn't

have been caught dead taking the bus.) At 10:45 there was another lecture, followed by lunch at noon and a third lecture at 2:00 P.M. Dinner was at 5:30 P.M. and the musical entertainment started at 7:30 P.M. Then it was lights-out. For the next five days, we were going to be living on elder saving time.

The last time we had lived as members of a group on a schedule was in 1971 at the Esalen Institute in Big Sur. There, Larry's need to be the exception to the rule was oddly tested. Esalen, the source and font of the human-potential movement, was a place where you were supposed to do whatever you wanted. You were invited to get into tubs with other nude people. You were applauded for pounding a pillow while berating your mother. You were encouraged to tell people exactly what you thought about them, "openly and honestly," in twice-daily encounter groups. Then you were supposed to close your eyes and fall backward into their waiting arms. It was a trust exercise.

Another favorite group activity at Esalen was the telling and interpretation of dreams. One person dreamed she was a storm trooper; another was a grain of brown rice. (This was California when macrobiotics were big.) Jungian dream interpretation was also in style. This meant that when you told your dream, you were *not* to say, "I *dreamed* I was a grain of brown rice," because that distanced you from the experience. "I *am* a piece of brown rice" is how you were supposed to begin. Rebellion under such liberal circumstances is hard to come by, but when it got to be his turn, Larry found a way. "I am a Peruvian dwarf transvestite," he began.

Larry does not like regimentation. He does not take well to incursions into his personal freedoms, like having to wear a name tag around his neck, keep to a schedule, be in a color group, or be asked to hand over his car keys. He doesn't like authority and he doesn't like rules. He's a lawyer.

Orientation was at 4:00 P.M. sharp in the hotel parlor. We showed up a little late and sat in the back of the room, on the side, from which vantage point I quickly observed that elderhostelers, with a few exceptions, do not dye their hair or get their faces lifted, two antiaging options that had recently crossed my mind; nor do they wear blue jeans that hurt when they sit down. They wear pants with elastic waists.

"We look younger than these people, right?" I whispered in Larry's ear.

My question was met with an ominous silence.

"No, really, Larry. I'm serious."

"Don't worry," he says. "You're the youngest woman in Elderhostel not on a walker."

After a few welcoming remarks and a stern warning—"lectures start on time"—we were asked to introduce ourselves. Most of the people in the blue group were retired. There were lots of former schoolteachers, a handful of professors, a couple of MDs, an engineer, a priest, a retired lawyer, and a woman who claimed she was a retired astronaut. (Later the woman confessed to Larry that she'd only said that because she was annoyed by the dazzling display of high-minded, if retired, professional prowess on display around her. She won his instant admiration. Larry has a warm spot for the misbehaving elderly.)

Eating lunch and dinner with the aged gave us an

opportunity to find out what retired people do. It turns out they work. The schoolteachers volunteer in the schools. The priest ministers to the sick and dying. The professors continue to write scholarly works, the doctors volunteer in clinics, and the engineers consult. In their spare time they build habitats for humanity and take piano lessons.

Older people are especially fond of outdoor adventures. They hike in Patagonia, trek in Nepal, and slog through the rain forests in Costa Rica, just like we did when we were younger. Rocking is out. So are float-and-bloat cruises. Warming your old bones in the sun won't do. Nor will teeing off, playing doubles, or visiting your children. It's got to be a "learning-adventure vacation." The new elderly work at play.

They vacation with a vengeance. It is not good enough to visit a Navajo pueblo, watch a Native American rain dance, have a nice southwestern dinner, and call it a day. Only the slothful elderly would visit an ancient Anasazi ruin without getting down on their hands and knee replacements for a week or two and sifting for ancient pottery shards. For vacationers too feeble to dig, run rapids, visit every state in the continental U.S.A. in a trailer, or sign up for Elder-Everest, there's always a fifteen-mile-per-day bike trip.

They seem not to want to stay at home in their own time zone, tend to their recalcitrant bodily functions, have insomnia in their own beds, watch travel documentaries on TV, and otherwise enjoy the rest that is their due after a lifetime of vigorous vacationing. They will not rent a house in Florence or Provence for a month and just hang out. They will not take it easy. Even at play, the new old are pursued by the puritan ethic. Some of them are on nearly perpetual vacation, returning to their condos or retirement villages only to do the wash, buy a new pair of Nikes, and repack. They have traded their birthright—leisure—for a mess of activity.

When it comes to intellectual pursuits, elder vacation behavior seems equally counterintuitive. Elderhostelers, we noticed, are eager students. In their second childhood, they go to the head of the class. They fill up the front rows first. They pay attention. They take notes as if there were going to be a test. They wave their hands to be called on. They ask interesting and informed questions. They keep the lecturer pinned to his podium after class.

When I went to grammar school, people who did that were called brownnosers. I know. I *was* one. When the teacher asked, "Why must I always see the same hands?" she meant me.

But would I like to go to school instead of on vacation? Do I want to attend three classes a day and learn for the sake of learning, when it's getting harder and harder to concentrate and I'm probably not going to remember anything by the next day anyway?

The year before, submitting to elderpressure at home, I had joined a reading group. (The other alternatives available to my age group—the perpetually late middle-aged—were joining an investment club or learning to play bridge.) The group took a vote and decided that we should avoid reading Oprahratic contemporary works and instead focus on the classics, books we'd either missed entirely when we were at school or had always meant to read but never did, and, as it turned out, for good reason.

Last summer's reading assignment was *Don Quixote*, 936 pages of tiny, closely leaded type. After 250 pages, and with renewed enthusiasm for *The Man of La Mancha*, I quit. Maybe I don't want to fight the implacable foe. (*Remembrance of Things Past* was also no piece of cake.)

By day three at Elderhostel, after faithfully attending lectures on American diplomacy in Japan, South America, and the Middle East, rushing around, eating on time, and earnestly pursuing intellectual enlightenment, we busted out.

Larry said he had a shaggy fingernail, so he had to go to the nearest town to get an emery board right away. I volunteered to keep him company.

"Turn right!" I said as soon as we hit the open road.

"Now turn left," I cried.

It's a game we play when we travel. The passenger gets to call the turn, according to his or her whim. The driver must obey. We first played "turn right, turn left" on our honeymoon. That's how, while on the road from Florence to Rome, we discovered the ancient wall paintings in Tarquinia.

This time we ended up in Jamestown, New York, famous for being the birthplace of Lucille Ball. There's a museum and a gift shop devoted to her memory.

"These older people are very admirable," I allowed as I wandered through the shop, trying to decide between the Vitameatavegamin refrigerator magnet and the T-shirt.

"Intellectually lively," said Larry.

"And curious," I added.

"Physically very energetic too."

"They don't even carry pictures of their grandchildren."

"They don't think about being old."

"They don't ever talk about their aches and pains."

"Or their doctors or their pills. They have a healthy outlook," said Larry.

"They're in complete denial," I said. "I want to be just like them when I grow up."

Epilogue

We have finally done it. We have rented a house in Provence for next September. For the entire month our home address will be L'Isle-sur-la-Sorgue. We made up our minds last spring when we re-revisited the town that had charmed us when we first saw it on market day in the fall of 1998. There we'd be again, walking arm in arm through the streets where we stood four years earlier and listened to the accordion player entertain. There was the bridge we'd crossed over the river—the very bench on which we'd sat and watched the huge paddles of an ancient wooden waterwheel, draped with vegetation, churn at the river.

One would have thought, given our record for fatal rental fantasies, that neither of us would have dared to say, "Wouldn't it be great to live here for a while?" But one of us did. I think it was me.

This time, though, it will be different. This fantasy is different because it has some reality built in. We're going to study French in France. It's pretty obvious by now that we're never going to take a Berlitz course when we get home. Besides, as everybody knows, the best way to learn a language is to live in the country where it's spoken. And it's definitely the way to break through the tourist barrier and make oneself feel at home.

Every morning we'll wake up and ride our bikes to the café where we're regulars and they like us even though we're Americans. Larry will smoke. Then, from 9:00 A.M. to 1:00 P.M. we'll be studying conversational French with Madame Desroziers, according to her "*totale immersion*" method. We probably won't get to be fluent in a month, but at least we are not going to be spending the rest of what's left of our lives circumlocuting the French language, groping for nouns and idioms until *les vaches* come home.

After school, we'll gather together our authentic Provençal dinners from various local merchants. Larry will ask them about the best local cheeses and wines.

We won't need a lot of stuff. The house comes furnished with linens and all the other essentials. We're each going to pack at most a couple of pairs of jeans and some T-shirts, and maybe something slightly dressy, in case we want to treat ourselves to a restaurant meal now and then. We want to slow down the pace of our lives. Mostly we're just going to hang around the house and take it easy. The place we've rented has two bedrooms and two baths, so if you think you'd like to visit Provence next summer, why don't you plan to spend at least a few days with us? No, *really.*